MW00490832

Praise for *The Pathway to God's Presence*

The Pathway to God's Presence will challenge you, stretch you and encourage you. Tom shows us that finding your way into God's presence is not a matter of dropping by for a few moments when it's convenient.

As you read this book, you will walk a path few have trodden. Yet, it is a path open for all who seek to go deeper with the Lord. This is not a "how to" book as much as it is a roadmap along the path of prayer that leads you into a deeper awareness of "His presence."

I love this book. You will love it too. Get ready! Your prayer life is about to take a turn in a new and wonderful direction.

Michael Catt
Sherwood Baptist Church, Albany, GA

Tom Elliff understands the pathway to revival as well as any spiritual leader I know. And his experience as a missionary and leader of the world's largest mission agencies adds urgency to his plea for revival. Spiritual awakening in the church is *the* critical factor for world evangelization [and] this book outlines the spiritual solution for our times.

Byron Paulus
Executive Director, Life Action Ministries

Some men write a book, but then discount it with their lives. Other men write a book and then illustrate it with their lives. This book fits the latter category. Written by a man who is one of the godliest men I know, this work is thoroughly biblical, intensely practical, and personally challenging. I started reading it in my chair and ended reading it on my knees, asking God to renew His glory in me.

Chuck Lawless
Dean of Graduate Studies, Southeastern Seminary
Global Theological Education Consultant,
IMB Connecting

The PATHWAY
TO GOD'S PRESENCE

TOM ELLIFF

CLC
PUBLICATIONS

Fort Washington, PA 19034

The Pathway to God's Presence
Published by CLC Publications

U.S.A.
P.O. Box 1449, Fort Washington, PA 19034

UNITED KINGDOM
CLC International (UK)
51 The Dean. Alresford, Hampshire, SO24 9BJ

Tom Elliff © 2014

All rights reserved. Published 2014

Printed in the United States of America

ISBN-13 (paperback): 978-1-61958-156-2
ISBN-13 (e-book): 978-1-61958-157-9

Unless otherwise noted, Scripture quotations are from
The Holy Bible, English Standard Version® (ESV®) Copyright © 2001
by Crossway, a publishing ministry of Good News Publishers.
All rights reserved.

Scripture quotations marked NIV 1984 are from the *Holy Bible,
New International Version* ©1973, 1978, 1984 by International
Bible Society. Used by permission of Zondervan Bible Publishers.

This Book is Dedicated to the Memory
of
DEL FEHSENFELD, JR.
1947-1989

Founder and President of Life Action Ministries
Having encouraged others on the Pathway, he now
stands in the Presence of God.

Table of Contents

Thanks

My wife, Jeannie, has been a constant pathway partner. Her companionship, dedication and spiritual insight are my life's greatest blessing. Marge Malone, who serves as Pastor's secretary at First Southern, has faithfully nurtured this project from beginning to end.

In Africa they say, "When an old man dies a library is burned." That is one way of saying that we are all storehouses of that which has been passed along to us. I'm sure that the contribution others have made to my life through books, messages and conversation will appear here and there throughout this book. Therefore, I am deeply indebted to all those who have been used of God to touch my life.

1

The Importance of Knowing

The lost sense of God's presence in a believer's life is an issue most of us are hesitant to discuss. We know that the moment of our salvation was accompanied by a remarkable, supernatural change. Paul described that change by noting that, "if anyone is in Christ, he is a new creation. The old has passed away; behold, the new has come" (2 Cor. 5:17). As newborn babes in Christ, we live with an exhilarating sense of God's presence. We have actually become a dwelling place for the Spirit of God!

But what happens when the "new" disappears from our relationship with Christ, and with its departure has also gone that special sense of God's presence? The question is not whether God is "in" us or that we are "in Christ." His Spirit bears witness to both of those realities. But what about those wonderful, spiritually tangible manifestations of God's presence? Is that merely a gift for the new or immature believer?

The Old Testament account of Moses with the children of Israel establishes a truth which each of us should constantly ponder: There is a distinct difference between God's provision and His presence. That sobering reality drove Moses into the depths of intercessory prayer. In that prayer, Moses acknowledged that the presence of God was Israel's only real, worthwhile and distinguishing characteristic.

"If your presence does not go with us," Moses cried, "do not lead us up from here!" (see Ex. 33:15) Tragically, the sad testimony of many Christians is that, unlike Moses, they are willing to plod onward with no sense of God's presence in their lives. While certain that heaven is their ultimate destination, they are both preoccupied and satisfied with mere earthly provision.

The world desperately needs the striking testimony of God's presence in your life. This book is written for those who eagerly, desperately desire to walk a pathway into God's presence. I am using the term "presence" to describe not only God's actual existence in your life but the sense of Him and His power as well.

We have established that Christ dwells within

every authentic Christian. So, if you are missing that sense of His presence in your life, you would first do well to heed Paul's admonition to "Examine yourselves, to see whether you are in the faith. Test yourselves" (2 Cor. 13:5)!

A careful and honest reading of First John will enable you to determine whether you are on that upward path, give visible or outward profession of that reality and possess the inward peace afforded every true believer.

You *Can* Know!

In the clearest of terms John asserts that genuine Christians can **know** they are in Christ and Christ is in them. Eight times within the five chapters of First John, we are told that true believers can know with certainty that their salvation is real (see 1 John 2:3, 5; 3:14, 19, 24; 4:13; 5:13, 19).

In the closing chapter of First John (5:13), John reminds us that a believer's certainty of salvation is the very reason he has penned the letter in the first place: "I write these things to you who believe in the name of the Son of God that you may know that you have eternal life."

How can you know? First John also provides us a guide for knowing the truth regarding our relationship with Christ. Consider the following evidences in the life of a person who is truly born again:

1. **Dedication to the Scripture** (knowing *and* submitting), 1 John 2:3–5. "And by this we know that we have come to know him, if we keep his commandments. Whoever says 'I know him' but does not keep his commandments is a liar, and the truth is not in him, but whoever keeps his word, in him truly the love of God is perfected. By this we may know that we are in him."

2. **Disdain for sin**, 1 John 3:6–9. "No one who abides in him keeps on sinning; no one who keeps on sinning has either seen him or known him. Little children, let no one deceive you. Whoever practices righteousness is righteous, as he is righteous. Whoever makes a practice of sinning is of the devil, for the devil has been sinning from the beginning. The reason the Son of God appeared was to destroy the works of the devil. No one born of God makes a practice of sinning, for God's seed abides in him, and he cannot keep on sinning because he has been born of God."

3. **Devotion to the saved**, 1 John 3:14, 18–19. "We know that we have passed out of death into life, because we love the brothers. Whoever does not love abides in death...let us not love in word or talk but in deed and in truth. By this we shall know that we are of the truth and reassure our heart before him."

4. **Declaration of the Savior**, 1 John 4:1–3. "Beloved, do not believe every spirit, but test the spirits to see whether they are from God, for many false prophets have gone out into the world. By this you know the Spirit of God: every spirit that confesses that Jesus Christ has come in the flesh is from God, and every spirit that does not confess Jesus is not from God."

5. **Deposit of the Spirit**, 1 John 4:13. "By this we know that we abide in him and he in us, because he has given us of his Spirit."

So how did you do on your test? In other words, *do* you know? If it is settled that you are indeed a child of God, an authentic Christian, but missing the awesome sense of His mighty presence in your life then welcome on the pathway to God's presence!

2

When the Glory Has Gone
from Your Life

". . . but I will not go up among you."

(Exod. 33:3)

Seated across the table from me was a personal friend whose life had both inspired and challenged me. The strained look on his face was underscored by the tone of his voice. His mannerisms conveyed a sense of fear bordering on panic, "I'm afraid the worst has happened," he groaned, "I just do not seem to sense the presence of God in my life anymore."

"Now, don't get me wrong," he continued, "I know I'm a Christian. I don't have any doubt about that. But there is such a deadness in my spiritual life that it frightens me. It really does seem that God has moved away. Perhaps He's taken His hand off of my life. Frankly, it scares me even to think about it."

For over an hour we discussed what had happened to him. As we retraced his steps, examining the spiritual decisions he had made in favor of his will rather than God's, it became plain to me that the "glory," that special sense of God's presence, was missing from his life. Now his most pressing question was, "Can I ever sense God's mighty presence in my life again?"

"I will not go up among you" (Exod. 33:3). It must have been startling for Israel to hear those words. The presence of God had distinguished Israel from all the other nations of the world. He had delivered them from the bondage and slavery of Egypt by His mighty outstretched arm. He had parted the waters of the Red Sea. He had provided water and food in the wilderness. He had promised them a land "flowing with milk and honey." Now He was removing His presence.

What had happened to elicit such a startling decision on God's part? What had incited the wrath of God to the extent that, barring the intercession of Moses, the children of Israel would have perished in the wilderness? Why was God promising He would continue to provide for Israel all they needed and wanted, yet He would not go up among them? And finally, a more personal question: How is it that believers today can continue on with the sufficient provision of God, but without that awesome sense of His presence, His glory, being manifested in and through them?

God had called Moses to Mount Sinai in order to give him both the Law and the blueprint for the Tabernacle, that beautiful picture of Christ in the Old Testament. But while Moses was on Mount Sinai, the Israelites, camping in the valley below, began complaining to Aaron. In the absence of Moses, and as far as they knew the absence of his God, they began to call out for Aaron to make them idols of gold. Aaron quickly responded. Soon, having melted the golden ornaments the people brought to him, Aaron fashioned a molten calf. The people began to fall down in drunken debauchery and revelry before the golden calf

The Lord instructed Moses:

> Go down, for your people, whom you brought up out of the land of Egypt, have corrupted themselves. They have turned aside quickly out of the way that I commanded them. They have made for themselves a golden calf and have worshiped it and sacrificed to it and said, "These are your gods, O Israel, who brought you up out of the land of Egypt!"

(Exod. 32:7–8)

When Moses came upon the scene of Israel's wickedness and rebellion, he cast the stone tablets of the Law to the ground. Striding into the camp, he burned the golden calf and ground it to a powder. Throwing this powder into the water, he made the children of Israel drink of it. (The object of our greatest delight, if anything other than the Lord, will always become the object of our greatest discipline!)

When Moses found that even Aaron was unwilling to admit his complicity in this heinous sin, he moved into action. Enlisting those who were on the Lord's side, the sons of Levi, Moses commanded them to slay every rebellious man they could find. By sundown about three thousand men had died.

Early the next morning, Moses called the children of Israel together and announced, "You have sinned a great sin. And now I will go up to the Lord; perhaps I can make atonement for your sin" (Exod. 32:30).

Moses then returned to Mount Sinai, where he poured out his soul in intercession for the children of Israel. And there Moses so identified with the children of Israel that he cried out to God, "But now, if you will forgive their sin—but if not, please blot me out of your book that you have written" (Exod. 32:32).

God's response to Moses' intercession was sobering. In essence, He would grant them His provision, His protection and ultimately their promised arrival in Canaan. But now Israel would continue on, with one major difference: "I will not go up among you," said the Lord (33:3).

It is significant to note that you can possess God's provision without God's manifested presence. Contemporary culture often confuses God's provision with His presence. The assumption is that God's presence can be measured in the amount of provision made available to us. In reality, even the nonbeliever has God's provision in his life. Consider the very air he breathes and the food he eats. All these and much more are provided by the hand of God, even though God's presence does not rest upon them. (Ironically, many Christians and indeed many churches have become so preoccupied with getting God's provision that they have forgotten the necessity of God's presence!)

Israel responded to God's sober declaration in much the same manner as my previously mentioned friend. With fear and trembling, each man stood at the entrance to his tent while Moses went out to the tabernacle of the congregation to plead with God for the restoration of His presence. Hanging in the balance was the one issue that set Israel apart from all other nations: God's presence.

It is the manifested sense of God's presence that distinguishes one believer from another. We often speak of that revealed manifestation of God's presence as being His glory. Yet, though we may glorify Him we cannot, in one sense, "give God the glory" because He already has it! His glory actually originates and emanates from His Person. The children of Israel often would speak of the *shekinah glory* of God, that physical manifestation of His presence seen in the cloudy pillar, or the pillar of fire, or filling the Tabernacle and later the Temple of God. When God's glory is manifested, no mere man can share the stage with Him.

The believer's responsibility is to glorify God. This means that we are simply to be in such a position before God that our lives serve as a platform for His majestic presence. This is what Jesus meant when He said, "let your light shine before others, so that they may see your good works and give glory to your Father who is in heaven" (Matt. 5:16).

Perhaps there was a time when you literally

magnified the Lord. In other words, the Lord somehow looked bigger as seen through your life. But now, you may sense that the glory has gone. Others can spend hours with you and never sense the presence of God. Your own fellowship with God is now strained and difficult. You look back upon the past as the "Glory Days" of your life. Like the children of Israel, such a loss of God's presence calls for a sober reflection and a serious response.

What caused God to remove His presence from the children of Israel? More importantly, what has caused the Lord to remove His glory from your life? The thirty-second chapter of Exodus offers a definitive answer to these questions.

Rejecting the Way of God

On Mount Sinai the Lord said unto Moses, "Go down, for your people, whom you brought up out of the land of Egypt, have corrupted themselves. They have turned aside quickly out of the way that I commanded them" (Exod. 32:7–8).

God had commanded Israel to worship Him and Him alone. Yet, now they were worshipping a golden idol. Is it possible you are aware of explicit commands of God from which you have deliberately turned aside? If so, like Israel, you have rejected the ways of God.

Once I received a phone call from a distressed member of the church I was pastoring. He said, "Preacher, I'm so confused. In fact, I don't even think I'm saved!" At his request I met with him to discuss his problem. Over and over he kept saying, "I just don't sense God in my life anymore. Does that mean I don't possess His gift of eternal life?"

I asked my friend if he would share the testimony of his conversion. He then related in no uncertain terms how God had found him and how he, by faith, had received Christ as his Savior. But now he was still left with this lost sense of God's presence. Of course, it was not my responsibility to give him the assurance of his salvation. That is the work of the Holy Spirit who bears witness with our spirit that we are the children of God (see 1 John 4:13; Rom. 8:16). But before I left, I did ask him to participate in one specific spiritual exercise. I encouraged him to go alone before God and ask Him to speak to him by His Spirit, revealing any area of his life where he was violating a specific known command.

The next morning my phone rang and it was the church member I had visited the night before. With excitement in his voice he said, "I need to talk with you right away." Later that morning he said, "Preacher, you won't believe what God showed me last night. He showed me that I was going through these days of absolute torment because of a specific sin I am committing." He then related the following: "Several months ago, I stopped practicing the biblical principle of tithing. I thought to myself that I just didn't have enough money to tithe any longer. I recall that almost immediately I began losing that sense of intimate fellowship with the Lord. Preacher, would God be using this to get my attention?"

As we visited that morning, I told my friend that, when a believer sins, God's Holy Spirit immediately begins to convict him. But if we refuse to respond to His conviction, then God begins removing our sense of His presence in our lives.

Now, just as we would be offended if we saw someone reach in and remove money from the offering plate, so the person is no less a thief who has resources belonging to God and fails to act in accordance with His command. That is why the Bible declares that those who do not tithe have robbed God (see Mal. 3:8).

I asked my friend, "Do you honestly expect that the Lord will look on a person like that and say, 'Well, there is one of My children who has decided once again not to obey Me; that child is not going to trust Me with his resources. I think I will really bless him this week with even more resources and a deeper sense of My presence?' God is more likely to respond in a manner that is precisely contrary. He may give us fewer resources to handle and a lost sense of His presence." My friend had already seen that truth before I finished that illustration.

The glory of God will be removed from your life any time you are unwilling to come to terms with Him regarding any known sin. Notice that the Scripture states, "They . . . turned aside quickly out of the way " (Exod. 32:8). This simply means they became very impatient with God. They were willing to try God's way for a while, but they had no life commitment to it.

With many professing believers, the Christian life is still experimental. They will commit themselves to a few days, weeks or months of discipline and devotion. But if circumstances do not rapidly change, they will quickly turn aside out of the way. After all, there really are other ways of getting what we want apart from God's way.

Notice also that the children of Israel received ready encouragement and cooperation from Aaron. You will always run into people who will tell you that everything you want to do is exactly what you ought to do. Aaron's morality determined his theology. His high-sounding rationalization of their corrupt activities was all they needed for the children of Israel to turn aside from the way of God.

Many people start out with good intentions to live by the principles of God. They will, for example, make a commitment to settle for nothing less than God's perfect will concerning their life's mate. Somewhere along the line, however, they meet and "fall in love" with a person who's life does not meet the standards for marriage clearly described in God's Word. Suddenly, they begin labeling those who clearly espouse the high standards of God as Pharisees, living by the letter rather than the spirit of the Law. And ultimately they manage to find an authority figure who will advise them that what they want to do is exactly what they ought to do. There is a marriage, followed by a few weeks or months of bliss. But then there comes a sobering awareness that there is a needed quality absent from their marriage . . . the presence of God is missing.

If the definite sense of God's presence is missing from your life, you should ask yourself these questions. Have I rejected the ways of God? Am

I living in open contradiction to any of God's known principles? Am I refusing to come to terms with God on any issue in my life?

Until you deal with these questions, you cannot expect God to trust you with His glorious presence. After all, if He cannot even trust you to keep His Word, what would you do with His glory but corrupt it? The blessing of His presence would send a signal to the world that you can live in disobedience to God and still have both His provision and His presence.

Refraining from the Worship of God

God registered a second complaint against Israel: "They have made for themselves a golden calf and have worshiped it and sacrificed to it" (Exod. 32:8). Israel now had a god no bigger than their imagination. Their human will and activities were subjected and controlled by an inhuman object. And most remarkable of all, they began trusting an inhuman object to give what only God was capable of giving.

When Israel's devotion was turned away from God, He threatened to remove His presence. Why should He commit Himself to those who had not committed themselves to Him. Israel's devotion and practice was reduced to the level of the nations around them. Their worship became an exercise in self-gratification. They "sat down to eat and drink and rose up to play" (Exod. 32:6).

The parallels here are frightening. If you are experiencing a lost sense of God's presence, you should ask yourself the following questions: Is there anyone or anything in my life which takes precedence over God? Who or what has become the greatest controlling factor in my behavior? What gets my greatest attention? My greatest time? My greatest resources? What relationship do I treasure the most? Is there some object or activity I actually value more than my relationship with God? After all, "where your treasure is, there your heart will be also" (Matt. 6:21).

Once, while seated on a church platform where I was to preach revival services, the pastor turned to me and quipped, "Man! I sure hated to turn the television off during the last ten minutes of that football game! But I had already stayed home longer than I should have! I was almost late to church!" How much of God's glory do you think he experienced that night? How much of God's glory do you believe He would trust to any person whose testimony was that coming to church was interrupting an activity he enjoyed immensely.

I once asked another pastor about his greatest

ambition in life. His reply indicated his desire for a particular level of achievement in a sporting activity. Golden calves come in many forms!

One cannot read the Bible without sensing God's desire for His people to come before Him in worship and praise. He deliberately set aside regular times of worship, special feast days and seasons and unique calls to prayer. The apostle Paul indicated that giving ourselves as "a living sacrifice" is nothing more than "spiritual worship"(Rom. 12:1). The popular "big business" approach to contemporary churchmanship may be nothing more than an attempt to accomplish with the cleverness of man what can only be accomplished by the power of God. But that power will never be trusted to those who do not enter into genuine worship.

For many people, worship is an exercise that takes place at a stated time during the week. During those times, meeting the schedule often takes precedence over meeting God. Interestingly, those who do not genuinely meet with God are easily impressed by others who have also never met with Him. For these people a worship service is judged by its appeal to the sensual side of their nature and little change is effected in their lives. The absence of God's glory is compensated by the presence of man's achievements. The statement "Woe is me," which so often accompanies a genuine encounter with God, has been replaced by the question, "Who was that?" upon hearing impressive preaching or singing.

God is calling upon us to enter into His presence. If we do not enter into His presence in worship, there is little likelihood that we will live in His presence throughout the week.

Renouncing the Works of God

Notice what the children of Israel said about the golden calf that they had made. "These are your gods, O Israel, who brought you up out of the land of Egypt!" (Exod. 32:8). Imagine the audacity of those people! Having been delivered by the mighty hand of God, they were now attributing that deliverance to an ugly idol made by human hands. How soon they had forgotten all the miracles of God. God is not apt to grant His glory to those who eagerly take credit for what only God can do.

I once counseled a man so burdened by a personal problem that he was ready to take drastic action to find the solution. He was so broken before God that he agreed to enter into a time of praying and fasting. He was beseeching God to move powerfully to bring about his deliverance. God, in fact, did move in his life and gave him deliverance.

When I heard about the man's victory, I called to inquire about it. Here were his comments: "Well, you know I've been praying about this issue for a long time. Let me tell you what happened. The other morning I woke up with a great idea. This idea was so great I immediately called those guys who were trying to pull the wool over my eyes and set them straight. I don't know why I didn't think of this idea earlier. They were so frightened by what I said that they immediately set out to settle accounts with me. By the end of the day, the issue was over."

I was saddened to think about this man's response to God's deliverance. By day's end, he was already taking credit for what God had done. It was, to hear him tell it, his idea, his boldness, his decisiveness that yielded the solution. Like Israel, he had created his "god" and now was bragging about how it had delivered him.

If you had entered the camp of Israel during those days and inquired about their deliverance from Egypt, they might have pointed to the calf and exulted, "That is our god!" They might just as easily have said, "Our old earrings delivered us from Egypt," for that is exactly what they were worshipping. They were bowing down to what had earlier been hanging in their ears, around their necks, on their wrists or on their ankles!

Is it possible that God cannot trust you with a sense of His presence because you are eager to accept credit for blessings which only His love and grace brought about? We are encouraged in the Scriptures to "magnify the Lord." This means plainly that through the lens of your life, others should see God as so much bigger than you. Unfortunately, we often speak so little of the power of God and so much of our own cleverness, that God is diminished rather than magnified in the eyes of others. Certainly God will not respond by giving us a greater sense of His presence only for us to take more credit for ourselves.

Resisting the Will of God

God leveled one final complaint against the children of Israel. He said to Moses, "I have seen this people, and behold, it is a stiff-necked people. Now therefore let me alone, that my wrath may burn hot against them and I may consume them" (Exod. 32:9–10).

To be "stiff-necked" is the opposite of being

meek. Meekness refers to the possession of a trainable and manageable spirit. The picture of meekness is of a powerful animal whose power is in submission to its master. A stiff-necked animal, on the other hand, may be powerful but it is useless. Such an animal will ravage the pasture land, drink up the water, take up space and attention and produce nothing worthwhile .

The essence of God's message was: "Israel constantly resists my will. I am unable to teach her. I have shown them marvelous miracles. I have given them mighty mandates. I have reduced them to despair and shown them my deliverance. Yet, they have, in a rash moment of selfishness, rejected My plan for their lives."

Is it possible that God in times past has given you a specific revelation of His will and found you responding in a stiff-necked fashion? Perhaps that revelation was a "call" to a particular kind of ministry. Or maybe He was showing you a specific path for your life. It might have been a matter as obvious as the divine impulse to go across the street and witness or a clear command to assume the responsibility for teaching a class. He may have instructed you to give a specific amount of money or to invest a certain amount of time. God may have instructed you to go to some foreign country as a missionary. His instruction might have involved breaking off an unspiritual relationship or reconciling another.

But your response was one of resistance. "I'm sorry, Lord," you said, "I'm just unable to obey you right now." Instead of obeying, you have plunged ahead in a stiff-necked determination to do your will, not God's. Is it any wonder that God will not give a sense of His presence to a person with a rebellious heart like yours?

In his book *Trumpets in the Morning*, Harper Shannon relates a story that speaks volumes about the consequences of resisting God's will. He writes of a young man who arrived on the college scene with the call of God burning in his heart. This student was brilliant, good-looking, popular and outgoing. Early in his college days, even the professors observed that, one day, he would certainly be pastor of a prominent church. His life seemed to have that special touch and his ministry, even during college days, was uniquely blessed of God.

The young man's seminary years proved to be as fully successful as his years of college. Admired by everyone, he began to move through the ranks of his particular denomination as one of those men destined for leadership. And once out of seminary he assumed the pastorate of a large church

that seemed to come alive under his leadership.
But at the zenith of his ministry, he just quit! It
could have been a "mid-life crisis." Maybe it was
burn out, but at any rate and for whatever reason,
he just "quit." Shortly afterward he assumed a
position with a large corporation. And with his
skills and his personality, he ultimately found
himself in the top levels of leadership. It was in
that position that he was one day challenged to
give sober reflection on his past. In the process
of interviewing an aggressive new salesman for a
key position, this man was showing him the ter-
ritory. As they drove through town, the younger
man turned to the older man and asked, "Sir, have
you ever made the discovery of knowing Christ in
a personal way?" The older man was amused by
the attempt to witness and began telling him the
story of his earlier years, his tremendous success
in the ministry and finally his decision to quit.
There was silence for a while, and then the young
man asked this probing question, "Do you ever
miss it? Miss being in the pastorate, I mean. Miss
doing what you know God wanted you to do."

The older man looked into the distance and
answered in the following fashion: "In days gone
by, kings would assemble their troops in the field
of battle. On the morning of the day the battle

was to begin, the soldiers would be awakened to the sound of the battle trumpets. Young man, I know that ever since I said 'no' to God, I have missed the sound of trumpets in the morning!"

I am hopeful that these pages will find their way into the hands of someone somewhere who has lost that sense of God's presence. The glory has gone. Perhaps, as that former pastor put it, you are missing "the sound of trumpets in the morning." It could be you have been so preoccupied with the cares of this world that only now do you realize that you have lost that clear sense of God's presence. You may not remember when it happened or how. But it is likely that somewhere in your life, you—like Israel—have rejected the ways of God, refrained from the worship of God, renounced the work of God and resisted the will of God. If so, my reader, this book is for you. For in it, you will find the pathway to God's presence.

3

The Temptation to Run Away

*"Now therefore let me alone, that my wrath may
burn hot against them and I may consume them,
in order that I may make a great nation of you."
(Exod. 32:10)*

The possibility of losing a definite sense of
God's presence is a sobering thought. No one
enjoys the possibility of failure. But a believer's
life, without the presence of God, is destined to
flounder. Christians are not immune to the pressures and strains of life. But the thought of facing
these without the certainty of God's presence is
chilling indeed. Yet it is at this point that many of
God's children are tempted simply to run away.

Someone recently observed that even the
Bedouin people of the Middle East do not change
their geographic locations as often as the American populace. We are, indeed, a transient society.
Looking beneath the surface, we would probably

discover that much of our external restlessness is the result of an internal discontent. It is as if there is something deep down within us from which we are trying to escape.

Perhaps it is an unhappy home, a poor relationship with your spouse, pressure from parents or friends. Maybe there is tension on your job. It could be that you are experiencing problems in literally every area of your life. The thought has occurred to you, If I could just run away from these problems or these people, life would be so much better. I could start all over again, and this time I would do it right. I would seek the blessings of God and determine to live in the very center of His will.

Rarely has any man been more legitimately tempted to run away from his problems than Moses. Think about it. Moses was reluctant to assume his responsibility in the first place. He never felt adequately equipped for the enormous task God had laid on him. Additionally, we find that his protests to God had resulted in a concession. Aaron had been assigned to accompany Moses. Now Moses' closest associate had betrayed God's purpose. Moses would rarely have won any popularity contest. He was assigned as the leader of people who were constantly bickering, exceedingly selfish and unbelievably forgetful.

Now as Moses turned the corner on a mountain path, he was aghast at what he saw. With Aaron's encouragement, the people had shamefully stripped off their clothing in the presence of their enemies; they were falling down in sensual revelry before the golden calf. At that moment God offered Moses a way out. "Let me alone," God declared, "that my wrath may burn hot against them and I may consume them, in order that I may make a great nation of you" (Exod. 32:10).

What a temptation! Moses could have run away and, unlike most people, he could have run away with God's blessing. What a temptation!

Have you so sensed the loss of God's presence in your life that you are tempted to run away? Are you thinking of leaving home, dissolving your marriage, changing churches, "throwing in the towel," quitting school, moving on, never to look back?

How should you respond to this temptation to run away? I would encourage you to follow the steps of Moses as he faced that overpowering temptation.

Acknowledge the People Who Will Be Affected by Your Decision

But Moses implored the Lord his God and said, "O Lord, why does your wrath burn hot against your people, whom you have brought out of the land of Egypt with great power and with a mighty hand? Why should the Egyptians say, 'With evil intent did he bring them out, to kill them in the mountains and to consume them from the face of the earth'? Turn from your burning anger and relent from this disaster against your people." (Exod. 32:11–12)

Moses' first consideration was the people who would be affected by his decision to run away. If Moses had refused to intercede, God would have consumed the people.

If you are tempted to run away, reflect on the fact that there are going to be other people affected by any decision you make. Those affected could include your spouse, your children, your parents, people at work who so desperately need a witness, members in your church, friends, fellow students.

Moses' first thought was not of himself but of the people who would be affected. Most people who are tempted to run away are thinking primarily about themselves. But Moses effectively put aside all selfish concerns. He ignored the customary concerns of his welfare, reputation or happiness.

It is so easy to fall into the habit of thinking about how little life we have left and how much good living we need to cram into it. I have talked with people who have protested, "My life is running out. I don't have much time left, and I have a terrible marriage. If I am going to have a happy marriage, it is surely not going to be this one. I've concluded that I need to find someone else."

Moses could have responded in similar fashion. He could have moaned, "Lord, most of my life has been nothing but trouble. I spent those forty years in Egypt as the adopted child of Pharaoh's daughter. Then running for safety, I spent forty years in the desert tending sheep. Now here I am trying to lead a bunch of ungrateful people through this dread wilderness to this so-called 'Promised Land.' My life is running out. Go ahead and consume these people. It's time for me to enjoy life for a change."

Interestingly, Moses could have run away without disobeying God. In most instances, people who are contemplating running away exercise great creative thinking to arrive at some "spiritual" or unselfish-sounding reason for their behavior. I have a pastor friend who has changed from church to church so often that he is a source of amusement to his friends. With every change, he has offered this hackneyed phrase, "Well, I would do more damage here out of the will of God than someplace else and in the will of God." I wonder if the will of God has actually played a major factor in his decision. It merely feels better to sound spiritual when you are trying to justify running away.

Often an unfaithful spouse will say, "You know, I realize that I'm making you miserable with my unfaithfulness. I know that every time you see me it causes you a considerable amount of grief. I love you too much to make you miserable, and so I think the best thing for us to do is to split. Why don't you file for divorce?" Here is a person trying hard to be "spiritual" about disobedience.

If the presence of God is missing and you are tempted to run away, first acknowledge the people who are going to be affected by your decision. A man once commented that his impulsive decision to run away seemed to be the best course of action at the moment. He lamented, "I thought when I walked off the scene, it would quit causing problems for everybody. However," he continued, "since my abrupt departure I have discovered my impulsive decision has cost everybody I love, and it will cost them for generations to come." The very people he left were those who loved him most. So before you run away, think about the people who will be affected by your decision.

Accept the Promises of God Which Relate to Your Decision

"Remember Abraham, Isaac, and Israel, your servants, to whom you swore by your own self, and said to them, 'I will multiply your offspring as the stars of heaven, and all this land that I have promised I will give to your offspring, and they shall inherit it forever'" (Exod. 32:13).

Without question, God addresses your present predicament in His Word. He has plenty to say about the decision you are contemplating. Here Moses was calling upon God to remember (as if God had forgotten) the promises He had made to Abraham, Isaac and Israel (Jacob).

The Bible is filled with wonderful promises for every area of our lives. Many of these promises are conditioned by our obedience to God's principles. Often when I am speaking to people who seem to have lost their sense of God's presence, they will remark, "Brother Tom, there was a time when I really believed God was going to bless tremendously. In fact, I thought He had promised me His blessings in His Word, but apparently I missed God on those issues. I'm not blaming God. I just think I made a mistake."

Psalm 119 repeatedly reminds us that God will give us counsel through His Word. He speaks to us through His Word and by His Spirit. It is interesting that people who are tempted to run away will often avoid places where they undoubtedly would hear the preaching and teaching of God's Word. Their Bible is no longer close beside them.

Perhaps it is rarely opened because reading the Word brings back memories of past promises. That is why David's most often-repeated discipline in times of despair was to recall the promises of God.

Moses is pouring out his heart here, "Dear God, my spirit is broken when I think of the people who will be affected if I were to leave, for you would consume them. But dear God, there is more at stake than that. You have made sure promises, and as a holy God, these are promises you are bound to keep."

People who are tempted to run away are

generally more attentive to their problems than they are to God's promises. "You don't know my problems," they will often complain. The fifth chapter of John's Gospel gives us a clear picture of a man who is preoccupied with his problems. For thirty-eight years he had been crippled. Now he waits at the pool of Bethesda for an angel to trouble the water. If he can be first in the water, he might be healed. He had tried to walk but was woefully aware he couldn't. His illness was not psychosomatic. Having been immobile for thirty-eight years his muscles, no doubt, had atrophied long ago.

Notice that Jesus asks the man a simple question. "Will you be made whole?" But the man is so preoccupied with his problems he doesn't even answer Jesus' question. "Sir," he says, "I have no man to help me" (John 5:6-7, paraphrase). There followed his well-rehearsed speech about why he could not be made whole!

Like this man, you may have built quite a case for your problem; for running away. Behind it all is the plain fact that God's presence is missing. Perhaps you even blame others for the loss of God's presence. Remember that a promise of God is more powerful than any problem you have.

Assess the Problems Which Have Prompted Your Decision

It is often the truth when we are tempted to flee, that we have merely failed to take a long, earnest look at the problems which are leading us to make such a decision. In Exodus 32:15–29 we read of several significant discoveries Moses made on the day he was tempted to run away.

One of Moses' most startling discoveries was in regard to his own nature. "And as soon as he came near the camp and saw the calf and the dancing, Moses' anger burned hot, and he threw the tablets out of his hands and broke them at the foot of the mountain" (Exod. 32:19).

Moses was not without his own problems. Once again his anger has surfaced! And once again his impulsive response costs him. You will remember that on his return trip to receive the Law, God asked Moses to carve out the stone upon which He would write. It would have served Moses well to have remembered the cost of impulsive anger. You will recall that later it is this same faithless anger that cost his entrance into the Land of Promise.

Moses made a second discovery. This one is in regard to his delegated leadership. It was Moses' insistent argument regarding his own weakness that caused God to provide Aaron. Then Aaron betrayed both Moses and God. In fact, Moses discovered that Aaron had considerable difficulty with the truth.

"So I said to them, 'Let any who have gold take it off.' So they gave it to me, and I threw it into the fire, and out came this calf" (Exod. 32:24).

"In other words," rationalized Aaron, "I am not the least bit responsible for what has happened here."

Moses also discovered the truth about the sons of Levi. As he stood in the gate of the camp he challenged, "'Who is on the Lord's side? Come to me.' And all the sons of Levi gathered around him" (32:26). The present difficulty was exposing character on every side. It must have been encouraging to know there were people in the camp who were on the Lord's side.

If you are reflecting upon the possibility of running away, you would be wise to ask, "What are the problems in my life which are prompting this decision?" It might surprise you how few if any of those problems would be solved by the decision to run away. In all likelihood you will discover these same problems will be packed away in your suitcase wherever you go. Your problem may not pertain to external geography but rather to internal geography. Instead of running away, you may need to make room in your heart for the presence of God. There may be furniture in your soul which needs rearranging—or even to be tossed out!

Activate Prayer for God's Presence in the Midst of Your Situation

> The next day Moses said to the people, "You have sinned a great sin. And now I will go up to the Lord; perhaps I can make atonement for your sin." So Moses returned to the Lord and said, "Alas, this people has sinned a great sin. They have made for themselves gods of gold. But now, if you will forgive their sin— but if not, please blot me out of your book that you have written." (Exod. 32:30–32)

From this passage through Exodus 33:17, we encounter Moses' great prayer of intercession for the children of Israel. Exodus 33:15–16 is especially stirring:

> And he said to him, "If your presence will not go with me, do not bring us up from here. For how shall it be known that I have found favor in your sight, I and your people? Is it not in your going with us, so that we are distinct, I and your people, from every other people on the face of the earth?"

Your life will never be without problems, and perhaps you will often be tempted to flee. But the major issue you must settle is whether God is present with you in the midst of your problems. Here is where your prayers are most crucial.

Praying is not the same as reading books about prayer or thinking about praying, saying "I need to pray" or asking others to pray with you. God will begin moving in your life when you begin praying. Like Moses, you need to fall on your face before the Holy God and cry, "Dear God in heaven, I need You to meet me in the midst of my problems. I am going to confess to You the reality of who I am and what I've done. I am going to lay my heart bare before You. You perceive the wickedness of my heart and behold what is boiling deep down inside. You know how troubled I am. I do not want to go another day without Your grace. Dear God, I need Your presence in the midst of my problems."

People do not generally run away while they are praying. Wherever you are, life will be difficult without God's presence. Wherever you are, life is worthwhile and exciting if in it, you sense His presence, His glory. His presence makes the difference.

Are you tempted to escape? Do you think the presence of the Lord will be more readily found somewhere else? Are you ready to throw in the towel, to yell, "I quit!"? Before you make such a drastic decision, consider the people who will be affected, the promises God has given to you and the problems you are facing. Then begin praying.

4

The Value of an
Interceding Friend

The next day Moses said to the people, "You have sinned a great sin. And now I will go up to the Lord; perhaps I can make atonement for your sin." (Exod. 32:30)

A careful study of Exodus chapters 32 and 33 clearly reveals that Israel's future hung upon the intercession of Moses. It was Moses who pled with the Lord not to consume Israel, and Moses who also cried to God to give Israel His presence, as well as His provision. These chapters speak volumes about the value of an interceding friend.

My mother was a woman who exercised great power in the realm of intercessory prayer. For a brief period after her death, I felt as if I were under satanic attack in virtually every area of my life. One day a friend offhandedly mentioned that I might be missing the effectiveness of my mother's prayers. After contemplating that thought for several days, I made a decision that brought profound results. Approaching three godly, praying ladies in our church, I asked them if they would undertake the role so capably filled by my mother as an intercessor for me. They gladly agreed. Immediately I sensed a clearing away of the spiritual oppression that hovered over me; and from that day on I have enjoyed the covering of their intercessory prayers.

A person who has lost the obvious sense of God's presence would do well to find a friend (or friends) who would be faithful to intercede for him. Israel had such a friend in Moses. He was so committed to them that on one occasion he exclaimed, "If you will forgive their sin—but if not, please blot me out of your book that you have written" (Exod. 32:32). And on another occasion, he pled with God, "If your presence will not go with me, do not bring us up from here" (33:15).

While we have many acquaintances who would be happy to "pray for us," that kind of praying is far different from the exercise of intercession. Therefore, it is important to select this "interceding friend" with caution. This friend should possess the five characteristics mentioned below:

Integrity

It is apparent that Moses possessed an integrity of character which Israel and her other leaders had lost. This is why the Lord had declared, "Now therefore let me alone, that my wrath may burn hot against them and I may consume them, in order that I may make a great nation of you" (Exod. 32:10). While Israel was playing the harlot in the valley below, Moses had been on the mountain, faithfully following the instructions of God.

People who are experiencing failure in a particular area of life often discover company with others who are struggling in the same area. It is imperative that the individual you select as an interceding friend be a person of obvious integrity. This person's walk and talk should come out even—because without integrity in crucial areas of his or her life, this person will be unable to intercede effectively for you. The psalmist states that those who ascend to the hill of the Lord and stand in His holy place, have "clean hands and a pure heart" (Ps. 24:3–4).

God presented Israel the Tabernacle in the wilderness as a picture of the various ministries Christ performs in the life of every believer. The altar of incense, located right before the veil separating the Holy of Holies from the Holy Place, represents the intercessory work of Christ. The perpetual smoke of this burning incense stands for the perpetual prayers of Christ on our behalf. When God spoke of this incense to Moses, He made it plain that no "unauthorized incense" was to be used (Exod. 30:9). The incense, in other words, was to be absolutely pure with no pollution. True intercession is born out of a pure heart.

In Genesis, Lot had an interceding friend in his uncle Abraham. The Lord, Himself, commented on Abraham's integrity. "For I have chosen him, that he may command his children and his household after him to keep the way of the Lord by doing righteousness and justice, so that the Lord may bring to Abraham what he has promised him" (Gen. 18:19). Out of his pure heart, Abraham poured such an effective intercession that Lot and his daughters were spared when God overthrew the vile cities of Sodom and Gomorrah. The value of personal integrity cannot be overstated.

Insight

Your interceding friend should have the God-imparted ability to see straight to the heart of a matter. He or she must have the capacity to be almost cruelly honest in pointing out the blind spots of your life, while at the same time being able to offer crystal clear scriptural counsel on how to overcome them.

Notice that Moses laid out Israel's plight and the cause of it with precision. "You have sinned a great sin" (Exod. 32:30). He accused Israel. Then in his prayer he spelled it out with an even more detailed explanation. "Alas, this people has sinned a great sin. They have made for themselves gods of gold" (32:31).

While acknowledging the precise nature of Israel's problem, Moses also called upon God to remember His promises. "Remember Abraham, Isaac, and Israel, your servants, to whom you swore by your own self, and said to them, 'I will multiply your offspring as the stars of heaven, and all this land that I have promised I will give to your offspring, and they shall inherit it forever'" (32:13). And then later, Moses prayed, "See, you say to me, 'Bring up this people'" (33:12). Moses' prayer illustrates tremendous insight into both the character of God and the character of His people.

God uniquely blesses certain people with a keen spirit of discernment. You will be miles ahead in your quest for the presence of God if you can locate a person of profound insight and willingly receive both their counsel and their intercession.

Interest

Moses exhibited an intense personal interest in the welfare of the children of Israel. There was a definite air of determination evident in the approach he followed. "I will go up to the Lord" (Exod. 32:30). Moses could have chided, "Folks, God is mad at you. I'm mad at you. I'm leaving." Instead, he rolled up the sleeves of his robe and asserted, "We are going to get down to business."

If you have lost the glory of God in your life, you must find a friend who is more than a casual observer of that fact, who has a deep sense of personal interest, who will take the time (and a considerable amount of time might be involved) to hear your heart, give insightful counsel and go before God on your behalf.

Some time ago I preached a message on the importance of an interceding friend. Afterwards, several people approached me about their pressing need to find even one person who really cared about them and their problems. "I don't have anyone in my life who cares and is really deeply interested in my situation." I heard that sad confession again and again.

In each instance, it was my pleasure to direct

these individuals to members of our church who had integrity and insight and would express genuine personal interest in their problem. Let me suggest that if you cannot immediately identify a person who has an involved sense of interest in your need, then ask your pastor if he can direct you to such an individual in the fellowship of your church. This is a true expression of the value of your church family. Many people have developed deep and lasting friendships during the "hard times" of their lives. Personal interest is not the only criterion for a true intercessor, but it is certainly a necessary characteristic, along with all the others.

Intercession

Moses gave himself to intercession for the children of Israel. "And now I will go up to the Lord; perhaps I can make atonement for your sin" (Exod. 32:30). Not everyone of integrity, insight and interest will be called to intercede for you. Intercession is a profoundly significant spiritual activity. An intercessor is one who reaches out and takes the hand of an individual who has a need, then reaches up to take the hand of God who has the supply and brings the two of them together. Intercession is as much the taking of a position as it is the making of a petition. It was Abraham, the intercessor, who, upon hearing of the potential destruction of Sodom and Gomorrah, "still stood before the Lord" (Gen. 18:22) on behalf of his family members living in those wicked towns. This is the kind of friend you desperately need if you are sensing God has removed that sense of His presence from your life.

True intercessors require a diligent search. There are many who will say, "Oh, I'll be praying for you." But more than all else you need someone to stand before God on your behalf, someone who will take your situation into his or her heart and hammer at the doors of heaven until God works the answer!

Identification

Moses was unwilling to separate himself from the children of Israel. "But now, if you will forgive their sin—but if not, please blot me out of your book that you have written" (Exod. 32:32). This is what the Lord, our great Intercessor, did, as explained by Paul: "For our sake he made him to be sin who knew no sin, so that in him we might become the righteousness of God" (2 Cor. 5:21). We are also reminded by Paul that, "even though Jesus was in the form of God, He thought it not a thing to be grasped, but made Himself of no reputation and took upon Him the form of a servant, and was made in the likeness of men" (Phil. 2:6–7, paraphrased).

The mark of a powerful intercessor is his willingness to identify with the person for whom he is praying. Norman Grubb reminds us in his book *Rees Howells: Intercessor* that Howells would often become afflicted with the same symptoms of disease as those for whom he was praying.

Some years ago, my wife was called upon to intercede for the husband of a friend of hers. This man was far outside the will of God. His life, morally and spiritually, was in shambles. At about that same time, we were spending several weeks in Israel. As we journeyed from site to site, I noticed that my wife would disappear for a brief minute and then return. I asked her about her strange behavior, and she replied, "At each place I am reminded of the great power of our Lord, and so I find a quiet spot, and there I ask the Lord, who has that kind of power, to move in the heart of my friend's husband."

True intercession involves such an identification with the person for whom you are interceding that they are always on your heart, in your thoughts and on your lips in prayer. All of us would do well to have an interceding friend.

Maybe you have searched and found no intercessor. I want to remind you of "a friend that sticks closer than a brother," none other than the Lord Jesus. He is "The Great Intercessor." He ever lives, seated at the right hand of the Father to make intercession for you and me. Even when you don't know how to pray, the Holy Spirit, with groanings that cannot be uttered, is making intercession for you.

Over the years God has blessed me with the privilege of numerous interceding friends, but even if I had none, I could rely on Jesus Himself, "The Supreme Intercessor." In your desire to have the glory of God restored to you, never overlook the value of an interceding friend.

5

Praying for God's Presence

Now Moses used to take the tent and pitch it outside the camp, far off from the camp, and he called it the tent of meeting. And everyone who sought the Lord would go out to the tent of meeting, which was outside the camp. Whenever Moses went out to the tent, all the people would rise up, and each would stand at his tent door, and watch Moses until he had gone into the tent. When Moses entered the tent, the pillar of cloud would descend and stand at the entrance of the tent, and the Lord would speak with Moses. And when all the people saw the pillar of cloud standing at the entrance of the tent, all the people would rise up and worship, each at his tent door. Thus the Lord used to speak to Moses face to face, as a man speaks to his friend. When Moses turned again into the camp, his assistant Joshua the son of Nun, a young man, would not depart from the tent. Moses said to the Lord, "See, you say to me, 'Bring up this people,' but you have not let me know whom you will send with me. Yet

*you have said, 'I know you by name, and you have
also found favor in my sight.' Now therefore, if I
have found favor in your sight, please show me now
your ways, that I may know you in order to find
favor in your sight. Consider too that this nation
is your people." And he said, "My presence will go
with you, and I will give you rest." And he said to
him, "If your presence will not go with me, do not
bring us up from here. For how shall it be known
that I have found favor in your sight, I and your
people? Is it not in your going with us, so that we
are distinct, I and your people, from every other
people on the face of the earth?" (Exod. 33:7–16)*

A friend and I were standing at the back of a
conference room listening intently to the
dynamic testimony of a young Christian leader.
My friend turned to me and remarked, "Boy!
He's really got it!" I nodded in agreement and
then whispered this question to him, "What do
you mean by 'it'?" "I'm not sure," responded my
friend. "But you sure know it when someone's
got it!"

What was "it" to which my friend was refer-
ring? In that particular case, "it" was that obvious
sense of the presence of God in a man's life. Some
might call it the "hand of God," and others, the
"anointing of God." At any rate, there is some-

thing challenging and appealing about a ministry that has God's presence upon it.

Is it not true that the manifest presence of God is the missing ingredient in so many lives and churches? And should not this recognizable sense of God's presence distinguish believers in Christ from all other people in the world?

Now suppose for a moment that you have lost "it." That is, you have somehow lost that sense of God's mighty presence in your life. The glory has gone. Life has become hard. Those tasks that used to be exhilarating have now become drudgery instead. Great effort is expended with little results to show for it all. Maybe you are beginning to wonder if it will ever be with you and God as it used to be.

The possibility of living the balance of their lives without the presence of God loomed large on the horizon for Israel. It was a sobering, fearful consideration. In fact, the dismal prospect of such a life was so overwhelming that Moses was driven to radical action in searching for God's presence. With trembling hearts we are going to walk through those days with Moses. We will open the record of his intimate conversations with God. And in doing so, we will learn how to pray for God's presence.

A Consuming Priority

It is quite obvious that, to Moses, praying for the presence of God was a consuming priority. It was not simply one of the many issues of his life. It was the major, all-important issue. To Moses, having the presence of God was as important to the spiritual future of Israel as having air to breathe was to their physical survival. Sadly, many people are keenly aware that the glory has gone from their lives. But they have yet to recognize the need for radical action.

I am reminded of the man who called me to lament the possibility that his family was breaking up. "Preacher," he moaned, "we're in trouble. Would you be willing to help us?" I expressed an immediate interest in his problems and explained that I would clear my schedule and that he could come in immediately. "Well," he commented, "I'm at work right now. Could I just stop by after work sometime?" To be perfectly frank that request left me cold. After all, if he had broken his leg at work he would have immediately gone to solve the problem. A broken home is far worse than a broken leg. It deserves top priority moving toward a solution.

Sensing the man's need, however, I agreed to wait at the church to meet with him that afternoon after his work. "Well," he hemmed and hawed, "Could we make it tomorrow afternoon? Today is the day our softball team practices, and I sure would hate to miss that." It was clear that solving the broken relationship with his wife and children was not the main concern of his life. Looking back, it is no wonder that their relationship was never mended. Big issues demand a big response. For Moses, the presence of God was the biggest issue imaginable.

The immediacy with which Moses responded to the issue indicates its importance to him. He returned to Mount Sinai the next morning after already having spent forty days there, interrupted only by a day of intense activity as he sought to cleanse the camp. Then, upon receiving God's assurance that He would provide, but simply not be present with Israel, Moses instantly resumed his intercession in the tabernacle of the congregation.

I am more convinced than ever that in most lives, "doing good" has become the enemy of doing the best. Our lives have become so consumed with literally thousands of little things—each good in itself—that we excuse ourselves from the one concern that is best. If your attitude is that the presence of God should be sought after you have tended to an endless list of other responsibilities,

Satan will insure that your list will grow increasingly longer. A lost sense of God's presence signals that it is time for immediate action.

That praying for the presence of God was Moses' consuming priority was also indicated by the actual physical isolation he deliberately established for this purpose. "Now Moses used to take the tent and pitch it outside the camp, far off from the camp, and he called it the tent of meeting. And everyone who sought the Lord would go out to the tent of meeting, which was outside the camp" (Exod. 33:7). It is apparent that the work Moses felt he must do in prayer could not be accomplished while surrounded by clamoring and calloused people. He wanted to draw aside and alone for his meeting with the Lord.

The pathway to God's presence is solitary. You must go there alone. That is a sobering thought, especially when you consider that Christianity is rapidly becoming "a spectator event." Like the thousands of spectators at a football game, we see and hear of the activities of others. We walk away from church worship services exclaiming, "We won!" when the truth is, like in all spectator sports, others won while we watched.

Often someone will complain, "I don't have the time to get aside and alone with God." The reality is that you have time to do what you want to do. And if you really want to get aside and alone with God, you will find a time and a place to do it.

Note the one issue occupying the mind of anyone going into the tabernacle of the congregation. "And everyone who sought the Lord would go out to the tent of meeting" (Exod. 33:7). Moses was going to the tabernacle to seek the Lord. On his heart was the issue of God's presence, not some provision.

It is often the case that our prayer time quickly becomes a matter of rattling off our hastily contrived and little-considered list of desires. The "things" we want are laid out before the Lord. Like Moses, we should have this urgent obsession on our heart: Where is the Lord? How may we receive the restoration of His glory?

A Clear Presentation

There were two issues on Moses' heart as he entered the tabernacle of the congregation. First, he wanted to convey his distress to the Lord. Surely this must have been a time of personal grief and confusion for him.

The Bible records Moses' perplexity, "Moses said to the Lord, 'See, you say to me, "Bring up this people," but you have not let me know whom you will send with me. Yet you have said, "I know you by name, and you have also found favor in my sight."' (Exod. 33:12). In other words, Moses is stating simply, "I am confused. You commanded me to bring up the children of Israel to the Land of Promise and now you have said that you will consume them, but bless me." Moses could not separate himself from the people or the task to which God had called him.

When you go aside for the purpose of meeting with the Lord, there is absolutely no reason for being anything other than completely honest. God knows your heart perfectly. He discerns the distress; He knows what is causing you this trouble. Many times our prayers are designed to gain God's sympathy, but He knows our situation with a perfect knowledge. You should state your distress as clearly as possible, "Lord, I know I've lost the sense of Your presence. I can't seem to will myself back into a more spiritual state. I'm both confused and helpless, and it's in this state of distress that I call upon You."

Moses continued by manifestly stating his desire. "Now therefore, if I have found favor in your sight, please show me now your ways, that I may know you in order to find favor in your sight. Consider too that this nation is your people" (Exod. 33:13). Notice especially Moses' desire to know the Lord. It was not unlike that of the apostle Paul who stated that his magnificent obsession was "that I may know him" (Phil. 3:10). Knowing the Lord takes precedence over knowing more about the Lord. It is a reference to that intimate, personal knowledge, the sensitive awareness of His divine presence.

Many people are satisfied with merely knowing "about" the Lord. Then, when they lose the constant sense of God's presence it seems to them that the solution will be found by storing up even more information about Him or accumulating more impressive theological credentials.

It is interesting to note that the most intimate physical act of marriage is often referred to in the Scriptures as "knowing" one's spouse (i.e. "he knew her as his wife"). But the same word is employed in speaking of one's intimate relationship with the Lord. This is a "knowing" that far exceeds factual knowledge. It is experiential and must emanate from our great desire to be totally surrendered to Him.

Some years ago in a college town, it was rumored that the quarterback of the football team had professed faith in Christ. The next Sunday morning the leader of the college Sunday school class in the local church saw the quarterback seated there with fellow teammates. Acting on an impulse, he called on this quarterback to lead in a closing prayer. The stunned young man, though quite at home on a football field, was less than prepared for this request. In his simplicity of faith, he stood and said, "Dear God"—then there was a long pause, and he choked out these two words, "You know." I am completely confident that God did know and understand his prayer. When you draw aside and alone for your meeting with the Lord, make sure that you candidly present to Him the distress of your soul and the desire of your heart.

A Committed Position

While in prayer for the presence of God, Moses uttered some of the most stirring words in all of Scripture.

> And he said to him, "If your presence will not go with me, do not bring us up from here. For how shall it be known that I have found favor in your sight, I and your people? Is it not in your going with us, so that we are distinct, I and your people, from every other people on the face of the earth?" (Exod. 33:15–16)

In essence, Moses had locked himself in the closet with God and swallowed the key.

There are two deeply imbedded and abiding convictions which Moses expressed in this statement. First, he was convinced that going anywhere without God is senseless. Anywhere is a barren wilderness without Him. Therefore, it would have been useless to move on if God were not in their midst. Failure to remember this basic principle will lead us to very carefully organize our lives, our businesses and our churches to operate without the presence of God. The machinery is in place, the gears are well-oiled and the measures of success are so humanistic they can generally be achieved quite readily by sheer human ingenuity and effort.

But God's overwhelming presence will so stir an individual or a church that all human tools of measurement quickly become obsolete. The early church, for instance, soon stopped speaking of additions and began speaking of growth in terms of multiplications. Are you willing to confess to the Lord your readiness to remain where you are unless He goes with you?

The second deep-seated conviction expressed by Moses was that the presence of God is the only thing that distinguishes God's people from all other people upon the face of the earth. This is an amazing statement considering all that God had done for the children of Israel. One might think that Moses could have looked upon the miracles that accomplished Israel's deliverance as the great distinguishing characteristic. But no. What set them apart was: "your going with us, so that we are distinct, I and your people, from every other people on the face of the earth" (Exod. 33:16).

We often give ourselves to clever designs and careful manipulation in order to gain distinction above others. Is it to be by possessions, by power or by popularity that you are known among others? Will you be recognized by what you have built or accumulated? Will you be remembered for your influence or your influential acquaintances? Moses peered into the heart of the problem. Our one distinguishing characteristic must be the presence of God in our lives.

Duncan Campbell was mightily used of God in the revival movement on the New Hebrides Islands in the early years of the twentieth century. While on a preaching tour in the United States, he shared the remarkable story of his conversion and subsequent call to the ministry. He noted that although God had moved in his life during his early years, there came a time when it seemed that the glory departed.

Having entered seminary, he began to question the veracity of the Scriptures. At that moment, Campbell confided, "I began to die on the inside." It was not that he felt he had lost his salvation, but rather that there was a dryness, a lost sense of the presence of God. During the seventeen years that followed, he continued to preach faithfully, later admitting to being nothing more than a "spiritual technician."

Having been involved in earlier, glorious days of revival, Campbell was often asked to speak at conferences on revival. He was also asked to speak on the moving of God's Holy Spirit. His speeches, however, were nothing more than perfunctory, and the power of God was gone.

One morning Campbell awakened to the sound of his teenage daughter singing in the drawing room. She had only recently surrendered to God's call to be a missionary. He slipped out of his bed and made his way down to the drawing room where his daughter, with face aglow, testified to him about her wonderful Jesus.

Then his daughter came over to him and said, "Daddy, I have been wanting to have a talk with you." Then her question struck home like a dart. "Why is it not with you and God as it used to be?" That is a question we should all ask ourselves, if it seems the glory has gone.

Unable to think about her question for long, he left for another speaking engagement. Upon returning to his home, he closed himself up in his study, telling his wife he would stay there until he had a meeting with God. In that room, praying through the night, God met again with Duncan Campbell. When he emerged it was in the power of God's Holy Spirit, and once again, he became a flaming instrument of revival from island to island.

Is it time for you to have a meeting with God, a meeting where you are consumed with the one priority of finding His presence, a meeting where you clearly present your distress and the desires of your heart, a meeting in which you express the committed position that you will refuse to go on without His glory?

It is intriguing to note the Lord's answer to Moses: "This very thing that you have spoken I will do, for you have found favor in my sight, and I know you by name" (Exod. 33:17).

That answer awaits all those who will meet with God.

6

Principle Issues on the Pathway to God's Presence

Thus the Lord used to speak to Moses face to face, as a man speaks to his friend. (Exod. 33:11)

"See, you say to me . . . but you have not let me know." (33:12)

"Show me now your ways, that I may know you in order to find favor in your sight." (33:13)

Setting aside the time to meet with God is a pivotal issue you must resolve if you intend to go forward with a renewed sense of His presence. Once you have made the decision to get aside and alone with Him, it is vital that you stay with the central matters in your quest for His presence. While we do not have the entire transcript of Moses' prayers for God's presence, we do have enough to illustrate these crucial concerns.

Communion

What a touching description we have of Moses' communion with God. "Thus the Lord used to speak to Moses face to face, as a man speaks to his friend" (Exod. 33:11). This was not a one-sided conversation. In fact, the next several verses indicate that Moses and the Lord were speaking with each other.

Above all else, your time with the Lord should be a period of genuine communion. I have been interested over the years in hearing people speak of their "quiet time with the Lord." Often it appears to be anything but a "quiet time." It is possible to have so many requests to take before the Lord that we finally resort to cataloguing them and placing certain lists before the Lord on particular days. That is both commendable and impressive! But only if time is given for the Lord of glory to speak to your heart. It is not a "quiet time" if you do all the talking and then race off to the business at hand without hearing from God. It is imperative that you wait quietly before the Lord, to hear Him as He has waited to hear you.

Two issues are worthy of note here. The first concerns the counsel we receive from others. Interestingly, many Christians still have the idea that life is divided into the sacred and the secular.

They believe it is extremely important for them to receive spiritual counsel only on matters that have spiritual consequence. On the other hand, they feel it is sufficient to receive secular counsel regarding situations that have no readily apparent spiritual overtones.

God, however, does not artificially divide the believer's life into the secular and the spiritual. Our entire life is to be an offering unto Him. It would be wise to seek counsel on every issue from those who seek counsel from God. We should be eager to hear from men and women who, themselves, are in the habit of hearing from God.

I have a friend who sought out the finest counsel possible regarding some persistently troubling financial matters. This well-known financial counselor was a successful man in the eyes of the world, but admittedly a nonbeliever. My friend contacted him because of his success, and with no regard for his faith. In the end, this financial counselor encouraged him to participate in some activities directly contrary to principles that are unmistakably spelled out in the Scriptures. My friend paid dearly for his failure to heed the Scriptures.

When we seek counsel from others, it should be from those who are genuinely wise.

Knowledgeable people have accumulated facts and experience. People with genuine wisdom have such a reverence for God that they submit both knowledge and experience to the scriptural standard.

The second issue concerns the counsel we give to others. It is equally important that we refrain from readily dispensing our own ideas to others until we have heard from God. It is almost ludicrous how ready we are to "shoot from the lip" about any issue. Friends who seek our counsel place a great value on it, even when it has not been the result of time spent with God. Your time of communion with Him will allow you to hear Him regarding those concerns that are heavy on your heart. It is imperative that you go before the Lord with as much eagerness to listen as to speak.

Conflict

Moses obviously was in distress of soul at this point. There was a heavy burden on his heart. On the one hand, he had received a command to lead the children of Israel. Now he was confused at God's readiness to destroy the very same people he has been commanded to lead.

> Moses said to the Lord, "See, you say to me, 'Bring up this people,' but you have not let me

know whom you will send with me. Yet you
have said, 'I know you by name, and you have
also found favor in my sight.'" (Exod. 33:12)

Moses was expressing in these statements the
crushing conflict in his soul.

Many people mistakenly feel that any pro-
gram initiated by the Lord will run smoothly,
unattended by any conflict. Yet, throughout the
Bible, we discover that conflict is often associated
with the accomplishment of God's will.

Listen, for instance, to the heart cry of our
Lord in the garden of Gethsemane. There was a
fierce conflict raging in His own soul. "Father, if
you are willing, remove this cup from me. Nev-
ertheless, not my will, but yours, be done" (Luke
22:42). We are reminded that there was such
agony in the garden of Gethsemane that Jesus was
literally sweating great drops of blood. Without
question it was a time of excruciating conflict.

E. F. "Preacher" Hallock greatly influenced
my life. When asked once what he considered the
secret of a long and successful pastorate, this man
of vast experience replied, "Fight every battle on
your knees." There are ample battles, but we are
to fight those battles in our prayer closet.

I have always been amazed at the composure
of our Lord as He went to the cross. There was

never a moment when He "flew off the handle" or "lost His cool." He always had perfect control of every situation. This did not mean He was detached from the conflict. He was simply able to walk calmly through the conflict because of what had transpired in His moments of agony there in Gethsemane.

The world eagerly follows people who have learned to walk calmly in the midst of conflict. They shine like bright stars against the bleak horizon of chaos and confusion. These are not people who are without difficulty in their lives. They are people who have learned to handle their conflict in those quiet moments of communion with God.

Your time alone with God will be marked with this kind of conflict—the kind experienced by our Lord who wrestled in body, soul and spirit. You will suffer agonizing moments, moments in which you express the sort of perplexity and distress which Moses recorded. And yet, this conflict must not—cannot—be avoided, but rather accepted in your quest for the obvious sense of God's presence in your life.

Conformity

Moses' chief aim was conformity to the plan of God and the person of the Lord. "Now therefore, if I have found favor in your sight, please show me now your ways, that I may know you" (Exod. 33:13). This is, after all, the main purpose in our meeting with the Lord--that we might be conformed to His image.

Those who know Christ as Savior soon discover that God has an eternal agenda in place to accomplish one basic purpose. That purpose is our conformity to the image of His Son. "For those whom he foreknew he also predestined to be conformed to the image of his Son, in order that he might be the firstborn among many brothers" (Rom. 8:29). It is worthy of note that the apostle Paul stated his "magnificent obsession" in words similar to those in Moses' prayer. "That I may know him and the power of his resurrection, and may share his sufferings, becoming like him in his death" (Phil. 3:10).

Now, God's agenda for your life—the order of worship by which He brings you into conformity to the image of His Son—will be different from His agenda for the life of another. But His purpose is still the same. He is conforming us to the image of His Son with whom we will co-reign as the bride of Christ forever.

There's a poem that captures this idea:

> When God wants to drill a man,
> And thrill a man,
> And skill a man
> When God wants to mold a man
> To play the noblest part;
>
> When He yearns with all His heart
> To create so great and bold a man
> That all the world shall be amazed,
> Watch His methods, watch His ways.
>
> How He ruthlessly perfects
> Whom He royally elects!
> How He hammers him and hurts him,
> And with mighty blows converts him—
>
> Into trial shapes of clay which
> Only God understands;
> While his tortured heart is crying
> And he lifts beseeching hands.
>
> How he bends but never breaks
> When his good He undertakes;
> How He uses whom He chooses,
> And with every purpose fuses him;
> By every act induces him,
> To try His splendor out—
> God knows what He's about.
>   —Anonymous

It is crucial to realize that God will work to conform you to the image of His Son in whatever arena He can find you. Perhaps because of your lack of a private "quiet time," you must learn humility through public humiliation. How much better it would be to grow in that Christian grace while on your knees before God in your special moments of worship, adoration and praise. God will meet us where He can reach us!

Some years ago a friend of mine asked, "Tom, has God taught you anything new recently?" That is a probing question which is sometimes difficult to answer. On this particular occasion, though, I had an answer ready. That very morning God had spoken to my heart on this issue of conformity. "I have learned," I replied, "how to get all I want."

I realized that such a statement sounded rather crass, cold and commercial, so I continued, "If I could just get to the place in my life where all I wanted for my life was simply all God wanted for my life, then all of my life I would have all I wanted and He would have all of me He wanted." That is the matter at stake in conformity--reaching the point where all we want for our lives is simply all He wants for our lives.

It is a fact that many people set aside time to meet with the Lord, only to waste that time with meaningless, thoughtless meanderings in prayer. Or worse yet, they merely order God around with their imaginations. I would challenge you to make time for a life-changing meeting with the Lord. And establish in your order of worship the elements of communion, conflict and conformity to Him. These are the principle issues on your pathway to God's presence.

7

The Vital Signs of God's Presence

And the Lord said to Moses, "This very thing that you have spoken I will do, for you have found favor in my sight, and I know you by name." Moses said, "Please show me your glory." (Exod. 33:17–18)

Serving as a pastor, I was often called on to visit patients in the intensive care ward of one of our local hospitals. It was not unusual for me to glance through the door into the room where the patient was lying, oftentimes motionless. From my vantage point at that moment, it would appear that the patient was deceased. There were no visible evidences (to me, at least) of life. However, to those attending the patient, there was an awareness of other indications of life which were not immediately, outwardly discernible to me. We often call these evidences a person's vital signs. They are the registrations of the functioning of the patient's essential systems. I have often been surprised to discover that a patient with no immediately visible signs of life can still have strong vital signs.

God's presence manifests itself in the believer's life with both vital and visible signs. In this chapter we will consider the vital signs of God's presence. These are those stirrings down deep within your spirit that indicate God is at work in your life. These vital signs will be evident to you long before the visible signs become apparent to others, providing a deep-seated knowledge that God is powerfully at work in your heart.

It would be difficult for us to imagine Moses' sense of joy and relief upon hearing God's answer to his urgent plea. "And the Lord said to Moses, 'This very thing that you have spoken I will do, for you have found favor in my sight, and I know you by name'" (Exod. 33:17). In other words, God said, "I will be with you." And from that moment, Moses began to experience the vital signs of God's presence.

What are these vital signs? Do you possess them? The following list will help you take your spiritual pulse. The presence or absence of these vital signs, by the way, should signal either assurance or alarm.

A Hunger to Know God at a Deeper Level

God's response brought tremendous encouragement to Moses' heart. Excitedly, Moses responded with this request. "Please show me your glory" (Exod. 33:18). In other words, Moses was praying, "I want to know you at a new level." Notice that Moses was not asking for more "stuff." He was asking to know more of God. There was within him an intense desire to experience more of God than ever before.

When our spiritual life begins to grow stale, and there is a lost sense of God's presence, we often turn to substitutes to replace that which has been lost. Those substitutes can be subtle, even possessing their own level of legitimacy. But they are still substitutes for knowing God. Hours of study, doctrinal orthodoxy, feverish religious activity and compassionate ministry to others are each commendable, but they cannot take the place of knowing God!

The Lord's response to Moses is intriguing. Simply put, God replied, "I can honor your request to a certain extent, but not completely. You do not have the capacity to receive all that you are asking. But I will give you all you can stand." Then God placed Moses in the cleft of a rock, covered him with His hand while He passed by and allowed Moses only a glimpse of the glory that remained after His passing (see Ex. 33:19-23).

When God restores to you the awareness of His presence, it will be accompanied with a hunger to know Him at an even deeper level than ever before. Do you possess such a desire?

A Definite Sense of Progress in Your Walk with God

You will remember, of course, that what transpired in Exodus 32 and 33 was actually an interruption in God's communion with Moses on Mount Sinai. Sin always arrests progress. If your spiritual growth has been impeded for a period of time, there is only one cause. Sin has wormed itself into a controlling position in your life. God must be allowed to deal with that sin before growth can accelerate. Once sin has been dealt with, then you may continue on in aggressive cooperation with God.

Observe how the Lord instructed Moses to pick up exactly where he had left off.

> The Lord said to Moses, "Cut for yourself two tablets of stone like the first, and I will write on the tablets the words that were on the first tablets, which you broke. Be ready by the morning, and come up in the morning

to Mount Sinai, and present yourself there to me on the top of the mountain. No one shall come up with you, and let no one be seen throughout all the mountain. Let no flocks or herds graze opposite that mountain." So Moses cut two tablets of stone like the first. And he rose early in the morning and went up on Mount Sinai, as the Lord had commanded him, and took in his hand two tablets of stone. (Exod. 34:1–4)

God and Moses were working together again! Within Moses' heart, there must have been that restored sense of joy in the fact that spiritual progress once again was occurring. What an encouragement to be back on the mountain receiving the instructions which would be so vital to the future of Israel, and indeed, to the future of God's people in every century.

As the father of four children, I had the privilege of working with them under all sorts of circumstances. It was amazing to note how greatly attitude affected accomplishment. When there was a reluctance to complete a specific task, that task became extremely difficult. Even a small task seemed to take long hours and much chiding. On the other hand, when there was mutual agreement and aggressive cooperation, even the largest task became sheer joy.

When God is powerfully present in your life, you receive the lift that comes from being a co-laborer with Him. There is a thrilling anticipation in your heart. You are no longer on a treadmill but are moving forward. You can sense the progress in your spiritual life.

Answered Prayer

Moses' request had been simple. It was two-fold. First, restore Your presence. Second, show me Your glory. Now read the account of God's response.

> The Lord descended in the cloud and stood with him there, and proclaimed the name of the Lord. The Lord passed before him and proclaimed, "The Lord, the Lord, a God merciful and gracious, slow to anger, and abounding in steadfast love and faithfulness, keeping steadfast love for thousands, forgiving iniquity and transgression and sin, but who will by no means clear the guilty, visiting the iniquity of the fathers on the children and the children's children, to the third and the fourth generation." And Moses quickly bowed his head toward the earth and worshiped. And he said, "If now I have found favor in your sight, O Lord, please let the Lord go in the midst of us, for it is a stiff-necked people,

and pardon our iniquity and our sin, and take us for your inheritance." And he said, "Behold, I am making a covenant. Before all your people I will do marvels, such as have not been created in all the earth or in any nation." (Exod. 34:5–10)

In other words, God quite simply had agreed to answer Moses' prayer.

It is patently true that you cannot have answered prayer unless you pray. When God's glory has been restored, you will be consumed with an intense inward desire to commune with Him in prayer. Each waking hour finds you discussing with God the matters at hand. It seems that every issue, large or small, all you face and every need is carried to Him in prayer. Over and over, you will find yourself expressing your gratitude to God for His answers to your prayer.

The most reliable barometer of your spiritual life is the extent of your prayer. The experiential presence of God in your life will evoke powerful prayers to the God of your life. Your prayer time will be more than early morning or late night one-sided conversation. Added to your specific hours of intercession will be the awareness that you are in moment-by-moment communion with Him. Prayer ceases to be a ritual you must complete in order to be spiritual. It becomes, instead, the spontaneous expression of your heart to God.

A Fresh Awareness and Excitement about God's Direction for Your Life

God distinctly reaffirmed His purpose for both Moses and Israel, "And all the people among whom you are shall see the work of the Lord, for it is an awesome thing that I will do with you" (Exod. 34:10).

Moses and Israel would become a platform upon which God would display His glory! Of course, it would involve high cost and tremendous effort. But both the cost and the effort would seem small in comparison to the new awareness and excitement about God's direction for them.

If God is dynamically present in your life you will be aware that He has a specific purpose, a divinely ordained plan for your life. This awareness will inevitably bring a certain degree of excitement in your heart. You will be possessed of a fresh desire to accomplish the work of God, as evidenced by Moses who then walked down Mount Sinai and, with authority in his voice, laid before Israel the majestic plans of God.

A renewed sense of God's presence will give a certain element of authority to your testimony.

There will be a confidence in your walk and a fearlessness about your work. When you have been in the presence of the God of all the earth, there is nothing to fear in the audience of mere men. An exhilaration will accompany the privilege of expressing the heart of God before mankind. You will experience a reverent excitement about His direction for your life.

Your Spiritual Desires Will Overcome Your Physical Demands

Moses' meeting with God on Sinai was nothing short of miraculous.

> So he was there with the Lord forty days and forty nights. He neither ate bread nor drank water. And he wrote on the tablets the words of the covenant, the Ten Commandments. (Exod. 34:28)

It is startling to realize that these forty days and nights were preceded by the emotionally and physically taxing days in the valley with sinful Israel, in addition to the previous forty days and nights on the mountain (Exod. 24:18). During those days the Lord must certainly have provided him with supernatural energy. What is more impressive, however, is that Moses' spiritual desires took precedence over his physical demands.

One of the most critical evidences of God's presence is that spiritual issues will become infinitely more important to you than physical concerns. This, of course, flies in the face of our contemporary culture. The world's message is that we must "treat our bodies right." But often more time is spent exercising the body than exercising the spirit. Though our physical welfare should not be neglected, neither should it take precedence over our spiritual exercise.

The apostle Paul made it a point to remind his physical body that it was not "running the show." This was one sign of God's unleashed presence in his life. "I discipline my body," he testified, "and keep it under control" (1 Cor. 9:27). He realized that the failure to keep physical desires under control could result in his being "disqualified" or not approved for God's use.

It is a matter of historical record that the men and women whom God has used mightily did not permit their bodies to shove them around. Neither did the clock! They bear ample testimony of missed meals and long nights of prayer. They are not readily drawn away from communion with God to participate in idle camaraderie with man. Their conversations with men and women produce great impact because they have spent much time conversing with God beforehand.

Not long ago, I heard the complaint of a young man who said, "I have so much to do, it seems impossible to have a good quiet time with the Lord." As we reviewed the "much" he had to do, we discovered just how often his activities were designed to satisfy physical demands and how rarely time was set aside to feed his spirit. We can assert with Jesus who commented during the hot, dusty noon hours of His life, "I have food to eat that you do not know about. . . . My food is to do the will of him who sent me and to accomplish his work" (John 4:32, 34).

Read the biographies of the spiritual giants, and you will discover they are a breed of people whose spiritual desires overcame their sensual demands. Do yours? This is a vital sign of God's presence.

How strong are the vital signs of God's presence in your life? Is it possible that some signs are weak or even missing? If so, dear friend, then like Moses, you need to find the mountain upon which you will meet with the Lord.

8

The Visible Signs
of God's Presence

So he was there with the Lord forty days and forty nights. He neither ate bread nor drank water. And he wrote on the tablets the words of the covenant, the Ten Commandments. When Moses came down from Mount Sinai, with the two tablets of the testimony in his hand as he came down from the mountain, Moses did not know that the skin of his face shone because he had been talking with God. Aaron and all the people of Israel saw Moses, and behold, the skin of his face shone, and they were afraid to come near him. But Moses called to them, and Aaron and all the leaders of the congregation returned to him, and Moses talked with them. Afterward all the people of Israel came near, and he commanded them all that the Lord had spoken with him in Mount Sinai. And when Moses had finished speaking with them, he put a veil over his face. Whenever Moses went in before the Lord to speak with him, he would remove the veil, until he came out. And when he came out and told the people of Israel what he was commanded, the people of Israel would see the face of Moses, that the skin of Moses' face was shining. And Moses would put the veil over his face again, until he went in to speak with him. (Exod. 34:28–35)

Vital signs generally precede the visible signs marking an individual's health. The same is true of your spiritual life. A person may be inwardly aware that God is moving in his life long before others notice that fact. But if God's glory is indeed upon your life, ultimately there will be certain visible signs of His presence. Moses enjoyed God's presence on Mount Sinai without the benefit of any audience but God Himself. Ultimately, however, he came down from the mountain to share what God had given him. It was then that all Israel became aware of God's presence upon Moses in a visible manner. What are these visible signs of God's presence in the life of a believer?

A Life Controlled by the Lord

Israel had been painfully aware of Moses' absence.

So he was there with the Lord forty days and forty nights. He neither ate bread nor drank water. And he wrote on the tablets the words of the covenant, the Ten Commandments. (Exod. 34:28)

Little is said about what happened in the camp of Israel when Moses made his second journey up Sinai. They must have awaited his return with fear and trembling, realizing that their destiny was somehow at stake. Then, forty days later we find Moses striding into the camp carrying the two tablets upon which God had written the Ten Commandments. It was obvious to all that God was definitely "calling the shots" in Moses' life.

A person whose life has lost the glory of God will often preface statements with such words as: "I probably shouldn't" or "I ought not to but . . ." or "This is not the kind of thing most Christians should do, however . . .". The very manner in which they speak of their activities indicates that they are not consciously submitting to the Lord's control.

Once I was sitting in a church meeting listening to a man give an ardent, eloquent and somewhat boastful defense of a specific action he had taken. When he sat down, a friend next to me leaned over and whispered, "Man! He sure is full of himself tonight!" That statement characterizes the individual who is missing the glory of God—filled with himself, but not the Lord!

I once heard a statement that beautifully describes the person whose life is controlled by the Lord. A small group was gathered to discuss whether they could convince a man to become the leader of a Christian organization. "Well," observed one man. "I can tell you this, you folks can go ahead and ask him about this, but in the end he's going to do what God tells him to do."

Can others expect you to have a similar godly response to the issues you face? Do the hearts of those around you rest in the confidence that the ultimate authority in your life is God?

God was in control of Moses' life. He was in control of his time, his diet, his activities—every thought, every motive, everything was in God's control. Moses rested his reputation with God! The closing chapter of Moses' life gives us this interesting insight.

> And there has not arisen a prophet since in Israel like Moses, whom the Lord knew face to face, none like him for all the signs and the wonders that the Lord sent him to do in the land of Egypt, to Pharaoh and to all his servants and to all his land, and for all the

mighty power and all the great deeds of ter-
ror that Moses did in the sight of all Israel.
(Deut. 34:10–12)

Could it be said of you that you know the
Lord face to face and that His control of your
life is plain to all?

A Countenance Which Radiates
the Presence of God

When Moses returned from Mount Sinai,
God was literally in his face!

When Moses came down from Mount Sinai,
with the two tablets of the testimony in his
hand as he came down from the mountain,
Moses did not know that the skin of his face
shone because he had been talking with God.
Aaron and all the people of Israel saw Moses,
and behold, the skin of his face shone, and
they were afraid to come near him. (Exod.
34:29–30)

The reflection of God in our countenance!
This is one of those realities that is difficult to ex-
plain, but which all of us have experienced. When
God is mightily at work in one's life, you can see
it in that person's countenance. When a person
has been with the Lord, it is written in the face.

Some years ago, I was seated on the platform

of a church waiting to preach the Sunday morning message. A door opened at the rear of the auditorium and through it walked a very striking couple. There was an unusual glow about their very countenances that indicated the touch of God in their lives. They were quickly seated toward the back of the auditorium. Following the service I met them as they were leaving.

I commented, "I have never seen you folks before in my life, but for some reason it just seems to me that God is all over you!" Smiling at each other and then at me, they related that they were visiting one of their relatives who was a member in our church. They explained that back home where they lived, their church was experiencing a sweeping revival.

"You know, Pastor," the man said, "our lives have been totally revolutionized by the Lord God. He is so near to us right now!" So it is with a person in whose life God is present in power! That person's very countenance will reflect the presence of God.

Occasionally, when seated on an airplane, I can recognize God in the countenance of the person seated next to me. Without any prior introduction I will ask, "And when did you come to know Christ as your Savior?" Not once have I been disappointed. You can see Jesus in people's faces when they are experiencing the greatness of His presence.

It is disturbing to hear so many Christians talk about how often they are tempted by others to indulge in sin. I have listened to men and women go to great lengths about sinful overtures made to them by people in their workplace. Often they speak of inducements to sensual involvement. It is my firm belief that a person upon whom the Lord is moving in power will have a countenance so filled with Christ that those around them would often shudder to suggest they become involved in any kind of sin. Does your face reflect the presence of Christ?

An Influence Greater Than Imagined

Notice that Moses "did not know that the skin of his face shone because he had been talking with God" (Exod. 34:29). Moses was unaware of the glory of God that was being reflected in his countenance. The result was that Moses did not push his power or abuse his authority. People beheld the Lord in his face and became more willing to heed Moses' words.

We live in a power hungry world. A huge question in most corporations is the question of authority. "Who's in charge here?" Moses realized how to wear the mantle of responsibility and authority God had given him. It appears that upon more than one occasion, Moses was actually surprised at the extent of his authority. He was amazed that others would follow him.

What Moses did not comprehend was that God's mighty presence in his life encouraged others to yield to his leadership. And what leadership it was! It is estimated that over two million people followed the Lord as Moses led them for forty years in the wilderness.

It has been said that "If you will take care of the depth of your Christian life, God will take care of the breadth of your Christian influence." We often operate in reverse, constantly fretting about the weight of our influence, when all along if we would go deep with God, He would bear witness to the hearts of others. Instead of gaining authority by force, by persuasive speech, by convincing argument and by exaggerated promises of success, we should simply allow the "Jesus" in us to communicate with the "Jesus" in others. When God's presence fills your life there is an influence which will exceed your wildest imagination.

After Pentecost, those humble first-century Christians constantly found themselves in the arenas, judgment halls, courtrooms and throne rooms of the world. In most cases those "captives" would become the "captains" of the moment. Filled with God, speaking words of truth with the anointing of God's Spirit and mightily attended with His presence, they would leave people spellbound, courtrooms in an uproar and kings in confusion. So it will be with you if God is powerfully present in your life. You will have an influence that far exceeds your imagination.

A Clear-Cut Sense of Mission in Life

Moses received from God the answer to his prayer for a supernatural display of His presence. With that answer, God also gave Moses a renewed sense of mission. He was to share with Israel all that God had shared with him.

> But Moses called to them, and Aaron and all the leaders of the congregation returned to him, and Moses talked with them. Afterward all the people of Israel came near, and he commanded them all that the Lord had spoken with him in Mount Sinai. (Exod. 34: 31–32)

Moses had a new sense of purpose. From that moment in the desert when God first spoke to him through the burning bush, Moses knew God had given him a clearly defined assignment.

But now, having met with the Lord and having received anew the promise of God's presence, Moses resumed that assignment without hesitation. He delivered to the children of Israel all the Lord had for them.

The saddest people in the world are those who are living without a definite sense of purpose. They have no mission, no ambition higher than to make it through today. There is no sense of calling in their life.

A wife once commented about her husband, "I just wish he would find out what God wants him to do and start doing it. For so many years, we have just messed around!" She was expressing the concern that is often hidden in the heart of a frustrated spouse. It appears that her husband's internal compass was swinging wildly and had done so for years. During those years she, and others, were paying dearly for his lack of direction.

Do you have a clear-cut sense of mission in your life? It is critical for every follower of Christ to possess this plumb line against which to measure all the other issues of your life. For a person without direction, "anything goes." Every idea receives equal consideration. Every possibility, no matter how ridiculous, receives inordinate attention. When every idea receives a "maybe so" and then again "maybe not" approach, it is more than frustrating! Do you have that unwavering sense of mission?

A Depth in Your Relationship Which Is Difficult to Communicate

There was one fact all of the children of Israel could agree upon: More was happening to Moses in his relationship with God than he could ever verbally express.

> And when Moses had finished speaking with them, he put a veil over his face. Whenever Moses went in before the Lord to speak with him, he would remove the veil, until he came out. And when he came out and told the people of Israel what he was commanded, the people of Israel would see the face of Moses, that the skin of Moses' face was shining. And Moses would put the veil over his face again, until he went in to speak with him. (Exod. 34:33–35)

It was said of a man that he was "a mile wide, but only an inch deep!" Every facet of his relationship with God seemed right on the surface. He seemed to share ALL he knew and ALL he was experiencing. Missing in his life were those experiences that were so deep and so awesome that words could not express them. Also missing were those moments so filled with the presence of God that, out of reverence for God, he would simply keep them to himself.

It is important for us all to be transparent, but the "what-you-see-is-what-you-get" approach to life illustrates a problem that is all too common. Many people have only a surface relationship with God. You can spend hours with them and hear not one spiritual expression bubbling up from the depths of their souls. It might better be said of them that "all you see is all they have."

When the children of Israel saw that Moses had the veil over his face, they perceived he had been with God. It goes without saying that all Moses had experienced was not easily shared. Moses, however, took great pains to convey all the commands God had delivered him. But how could he speak of those intense moments of reverential awe when God was so bathing him with His presence that his face would shine for days afterwards?

Pastors who lose the glory of God quickly discover this problem in their sermon preparation. Those who are walking with a genuine sense of God's presence find it difficult to restrain their thoughts and insights about the Scriptures. They are literally overflowing with information, and they share what they know with a kind of zeal that indicates, "Oh, but there is so much more I wish I could show you!"

When you meet with God, a quiet revolution occurs in your life. His presence overwhelms you. The Word of God comes alive. Your heart and your mouth are filled with adoration and praise. People will know you have been with Him, and yet your words are inadequate to express what is going on in the depths of your spirit. There is truly a river of living water flowing in your spirit. David must have known this experience for he often exclaimed, "Oh sing to the Lord a new song!" It was obvious that the same old words and phrases could not adequately express the depth of his relation with God.

Is there more to you spiritually than meets the eye? One of the visible signs of God's presence is a relationship much deeper than you can express.

After Peter and John healed the lame man at the Beautiful Gate, there was such a tumult that the Sadducees imprisoned them. The next morning they were hauled before the high priest. At that moment Peter, filled with the Holy Spirit, eloquently defended the miraculous work of God. "Now when they saw the boldness of Peter and

John, and perceived that they were uneducated, common men, they were astonished. And they recognized that they had been with Jesus" (Acts 4:13).

The fact that these "nobodies" had become powerful, influential "somebodies" could be attributed to only one reason: Peter and John "had been with Jesus." It was this fact that attracted the attention of those Jewish religionists.

Are there any visible signs of the presence of God in your life? Are others taken with an awareness that you have been with Jesus?

9

Going on in the Glory of God

So Moses finished the work. Then the cloud covered the tent of meeting, and the glory of the Lord filled the tabernacle. And Moses was not able to enter the tent of meeting because the cloud settled on it, and the glory of the Lord filled the tabernacle. Throughout all their journeys, whenever the cloud was taken up from over the tabernacle, the people of Israel would set out. But if the cloud was not taken up, then they did not set out till the day that it was taken up. For the cloud of the Lord was on the tabernacle by day, and fire was in it by night, in the sight of all the house of Israel throughout all their journeys. (Exod. 40:33–38)

Meeting with God and experiencing the overwhelming sense of His presence will leave you forever changed. But how can you continue to go on in His glory—that is, to con-

tinue walking with that sense of His presence in
your life.

We have noted that a person who has lost
the glory of God should take specific steps to
recover that divine sense of His presence. By the
same token, the person who has recovered that
once-departed sense of God's presence should take
definite steps to continue on in intimate fellowship with Him. In the closing chapters of Exodus,
these necessary steps are clearly delineated for us.

Acknowledge the People God Has Placed in Your Life to Give Sound, Spiritual Leadership

God goes to great lengths to place people in
our lives for the purpose of giving us spiritual
counsel and direction. These people may come
from among our family members or friends. They
may be church leaders or others in whom God is
manifestly at work. God often uses such people to
give us wise counsel, encouragement and spiritual
exhortation.

The closing six chapters of Exodus reveal
the stirring account of Israel's obedient action in
the construction and erection of the tabernacle.
The children of Israel willingly received instruction from Moses because they recognized he
was receiving his instruction from God. His life

revealed the visible signs of God's presence. Deep within his heart there were the strong, vital signs of God's presence. His life was characterized by those qualities we seek in an interceding friend.

Over the years, God has mightily blessed me with individuals who have shared sound spiritual counsel. Until I told them, many of these people did not have the slightest idea how important they were to me. They affected my life by the quiet example of their lives. Others have not only lived an exemplary life before me, but they have offered me important counsel at crucial moments.

Though you might have to look for them, I am confident that God has placed people like this on your pathway as well. Perhaps they are people in positions of authority and leadership, or they may be close friends who are ready to offer wisdom and understanding. You can detect God in their lives, and His wisdom and love are expressed through their counsel. Sometimes what they say may seem almost brutally frank, but "faithful are the wounds of a friend" (Prov. 27:6).

Have you noticed that some individuals express a "lone-wolf" kind of Christianity. They are unwilling to receive counsel from anyone. They are skeptical of everyone's ideas except their own.

No one is holy enough for them. Unlike Paul, they consider themselves to have arrived. How sad life must be for them!

It was never God's plan for us to operate with total independence from others in the body of Christ. The book of Proverbs abounds with admonitions to seek sage spiritual counsel from others. If others are not immediately available to you, then begin praying now that God will place in your life individuals who will provide solid, spiritual leadership.

Adopt the Practice God Has Given to Remind Us of the Importance of His Presence

Of all that God had given Moses on Mount Sinai, there was one issue of such importance that Moses immediately shared it with the children of Israel.

> Moses assembled all the congregation of the people of Israel and said to them, "These are the things that the Lord has commanded you to do. Six days work shall be done, but on the seventh day you shall have a Sabbath of solemn rest, holy to the Lord. Whoever does any work on it shall be put to death. You shall kindle no fire in all your dwelling places on the Sabbath day." (Exod. 35:1–3)

Why did Moses' first communication with the children of Israel involve the institution of the Sabbath day—the day of rest? Moses could have spoken about the construction of the tabernacle. Or he could have touched on any of the other commandments God had given him. But we must not miss the fact that when Moses returned from Sinai with his face aglow that his first words regarded the Sabbath.

One has only to remember, however, that the children of Israel had just been saved from suffering death as a result of their disobedience. They had forgotten the priority of serving God. Now God was saying to them, "I am going to give you a specific practice that will be a constant reminder of My presence. On one day out of every seven, I want you to give yourself particularly to seeking My face."

The word "Sabbath" means rest. It is an interruption, a stop, like a pause in music. God was saying, "I want there to be one twenty-four-hour period that you totally give to Me. In it, you are to worship Me. In it, you are to contemplate Who I am and how important My presence is to you."

This practice, the observance of one day of worship out of every seven, has long since been neglected by believers. Because of this it is no wonder that so many believers gradually lose their sense of God's presence. Notice God was not asking merely for a sabbath morning or a sabbath evening. God was and is asking for them (and us) to give an entire day to Him.

A wife was totally frustrated in her attempts to have meaningful communion with her husband. She related one particularly telling incident. Throughout the week, she had spoken to her husband of the need to talk with him about some important issues facing their children.

"I just need to talk with you," she repeatedly urged. But her husband stated that at the end of the week, when his work load was lighter and his mind could concentrate on the family, he would be eager to spend time with her. That Friday afternoon when he came home from work, she had made preparation to spend the evening at home with him. His response brought grief to her heart: "I had planned to spend this evening with the guys at the bowling alley."

The man had an insistent wife! "Then could we just spend some time tomorrow evening?" His response was, "Well, I'm going to a football game tomorrow, and I'm sure I won't be able to return until late at night!"

Now do you think spending time with his wife was a priority in this man's life? Obviously not. Do you think she would have good reason to question whether he genuinely loved her and cared to hear what was on her heart? Certainly she would.

The Lord is speaking to us through Israel's experience, through the commandment and through His own earthly example. He is saying "I want you to give one day out of your week to Me. On that day, I want you to worship Me. I want us to spend time together. I want to know that I have your undivided attention. I know you visit with Me each morning and evening and sometimes during the day, but I want this concentrated period of time with Me. And what is more, you need it desperately. I have made this command for your benefit."

How it must grieve the Lord to hear our response. "This is the only day I have to get work done around the home. This is the day I had planned for my favorite recreation. Oh, I may be in church and Bible study on Sunday morning, but that is not the only place where I can worship." Worse yet would be to hear: "But I'm so busy with the work of God that I don't have time for the worship of God."

Long ago, I made faithful attendance in worship a prerequisite for those with whom I counseled. There is no way for anyone to gain spiritual wholeness apart from corporate worship. What needs to be accomplished in our lives will only be achieved when we set aside time to focus our attention on God, both corporately and individually. If people are unwilling to set aside one day a week to worship God, what possibility is there that their problems will be solved by a private audience with some minister for one hour? Most people I know whose lives are constantly in turmoil are those who ignore the principle of God's Sabbath.

Do you hear what God is saying? "I want to see your face. I want to know your heart is turned toward Me. You want My presence in your life. You want My glory. Then I need your undivided attention at least one day out of every seven."

Act on the Projects God Designs to Test Your Heart and Increase Your Fellowship with Him

God assigned the children of Israel a specific project which served to test their hearts and to increase their fellowship with Him. This project was the construction of the tabernacle.

Moses said to all the congregation of the people of Israel, "This is the thing that the Lord has commanded. Take from among you a contribution to the Lord. (Exod. 35:4–5)

Mark the difference between this command and the command regarding the Sabbath. The Sabbath was nonoptional. In fact, whoever violated the Sabbath was to be put to death. The offering taken for the construction of the tabernacle, on the other hand, was to be only from those who had a willing heart. With this, God would reveal the true motivation of the children of Israel. He was going to test their hearts. Were they doing what they did simply because they would suffer severe consequences if they refused, or was there a deeper level of motivation? Would they be motivated out of love to bring an offering for the construction of the tabernacle?

This construction project presented an interesting situation. The children of Israel would not be disobeying God if they did not contribute, but their participation (or lack of it) would reveal much about them. You will note that the emphasis in the following verses is that the offering was to be brought by those with a willing heart.

Exodus 35:21: "And they came, everyone whose heart stirred him, and everyone whose spirit moved him."

Exodus 35:22: "So they came, both men and women. All who were of a willing heart..."

Exodus 35:26: "All the women whose hearts stirred them . . ."

Exodus 35:29: "All the men and women, the people of Israel, whose heart moved them to bring anything . . . brought it as a freewill offering to the Lord."

God gives us similar opportunities, special projects which will test our hearts and provide an opportunity to walk in deeper fellowship with Him. A failure to respond shows an independent disregard for God, an insensitivity to His heart. These projects may involve giving, serving and ministering. They may consume our time, our resources and our energy, but in each instance our hearts will be tested and our fellowship can be increased.

At Thanksgiving time, my wife once asked me to "test the turkey." She handed me a long, pointed metal tube which had a thermometer attached at one end. Then she instructed me to stick the tube right into the deepest part of the turkey. When I asked her the purpose of this exercise, she replied, "I want to know if it's as hot on the inside as it is on the outside." The Lord is constantly testing us to see if our spiritual temperature is the same inside and out. He is saying, "It is important for you to come before Me on the Sabbath as I have commanded. This will remind you of My presence. But it is also revealing when you voluntarily present yourself to Me, eagerly participating in a special project I have given you."

Act on the projects God has designed to test your heart and increase your fellowship with Him.

Accept the Part God Has Assigned You in His Family

Two men surfaced to guide the building of the tabernacle.

> Then Moses said to the people of Israel, "See, the Lord has called by name Bezalel the son of Uri, son of Hur, of the tribe of Judah; and he has filled him with the Spirit of God, with skill, with intelligence, with knowledge, and with all craftsmanship, to devise artistic designs, to work in gold and silver and bronze, in cutting stones for setting, and in carving wood, for work in every skilled craft. And he has inspired him to teach, both him and Oholiab the son of Ahisamach of the tribe of Dan. He has filled them with skill to do every sort of work done by an engraver or by

a designer or by an embroiderer in blue and
purple and scarlet yarns and fine twined linen,
or by a weaver—by any sort of workman or
skilled designer. (Exod. 35:30–35)

No one can do everything equally well. But
here is the good news: No one is supposed to do
everything equally well! God has designed each of
us with our own unique abilities, our heritage, our
testimony and our gifts with the purpose that we
might fit together into His family. In Moses' case,
God had appointed Bezalel and Oholiab. The
people brought their willing offering to Moses.
He, in turn, placed it under the supervision of
those two men. There were those who gave, those
who administered the funds, others who carefully
examined the blueprint for the tabernacle, others
who knew how to supervise the work and still
others who could do the elaborate, technical work
building the tabernacle. Each person assumed the
particular role God designed for him.

Many people lose the sense of God's presence
when they enter into a work God has never assigned to them. Perhaps the task they are attempt-
ing is noble and right. The only problem is, it is
not the task God has assigned to them.

I was acquainted with a man who was absolutely alive in Christ. It was easy to tell that the

glory of God was on him. He was a fine businessman and an effective Sunday school teacher in his church. But somewhere along the way, he became disappointed with his pastor. Then he decided he would prove his ability by assuming the responsibilities of a pastor himself. He answered a call to pastor a small church. The moment that happened, God distanced Himself from this man. It wasn't long before he was disillusioned and thoroughly disgusted with the church. He became cynical and critical, distancing himself from other believers.

In a similar fashion, a pastor friend of mine grew weary with his church responsibilities and announced his resignation to assume a position with a local corporation. In less than a month, this fellow was no better off than the pastor previously mentioned—dissatisfied, disgusted and obviously missing the glory.

It is important for us to operate in the area of our spiritual gift and in the particular role God assigns to each of us. Some years ago, I was visited by a pastor search committee. As we talked together, I asked one of the men about his involvement in his church. "Oh," he kind of boasted, "I am up at the church all the time. I head up everything I can. In fact, I'll tell you what: if I had my way I

would serve on every committee in the church."
I made a mental note that, should God call me
to that church, I was going to keep my eye on
that man!

It is a false assumption that the entire weight
of any church ministry rests upon your shoulders.
You are a part of the body of Christ, but you func-
tion as only a part of the body. You, with your
unique gifts, are designed to fit together with
others in your local congregation, so the work of
Christ might be done as a corporate effort.

Aaron is a perfect example of what happens
when an individual assumes responsibilities not
suited to him. In fact, the reason the children of
Israel were under God's discipline is quite simple.
Aaron assumed a role never designated to him.
While Moses was up on Mount Sinai, Aaron,
second in command, was to keep watch over the
people. He had not been given the responsibility
for leading the Israelites in a different kind of
worship. But when the people pressed him to
make a graven image, Aaron complied. He melted
down the gold, sculpted the golden calf, assumed
a responsibility that had never been designated to
him and led a nation into idolatry.

It is urgent for you to come before God and
find out how He wants you to fit into the body of

Christ, and use your unique gifts to make a valuable contribution. It is often the case that those in any congregation who are "worn to a frazzle," "ready to bail out," exasperated and experiencing spiritual burnout, have simply undertaken responsibilities God never designed for them. So accept the role God has assigned you in His family.

Abide by the Plans God Prescribes for His Work

The final chapters of Exodus (36–40) reveal the meticulous attention given to the construction of the tabernacle. God had carefully related detailed instructions for the tabernacle. Bezalel, Oholiab and the others involved rigidly followed those instructions.

We might ask, Why didn't they just build a tent and use it to worship the Lord? The answer is quite clear. Every aspect of the tabernacle represented a particular element in the ministry of Christ. The colors, the types of cloth, the particular metals, even the dimensions all speak volumes about the ministry of Christ in the life of a believer. It was essential for those men to abide strictly by the plans God provided for the work.

Scripture records that after the tabernacle was constructed and worship in it had begun, Aaron's sons, Nadab and Abihu, lost their lives at the hand of God because they disobeyed His commandment regarding the fire by which the incense was to be kindled. That fire was to have originated directly from the altar of sacrifice. This was to indicate that our Lord's ability to intercede for us (as pictured by the incense) was based upon the fact that He had laid down His life for us. Nadab and Abihu offered "unauthorized fire." Not only did the glory depart from their lives, but they lost their lives as well (see Num. 3:2-4).

If you want to lose the awesome sense of God's presence in your life, just try anything your way instead of God's way. It is not enough just to do God's work; God's work must be done His way. God clearly sets forth in the Scriptures the principles by which we are to conduct every aspect of our lives. These are not optional or alternative ways for doing the work of God. They are the immutable principles of our holy God.

A well-meaning Christian sought counsel in his attempt to reconcile two Christian brothers. He was reminded that the Bible clearly speaks about the procedure he should follow. He responded, "I really don't have time to get as involved as all that. I think I'll just do it as I had originally planned. At any rate, since I'm trying to do something I know God approves of, I'm sure He'll bless it." Later he lamented what an absolute failure his efforts had been. As a matter of fact, the irritation between the two parties had only been intensified; now my friend found himself grossly misunderstood.

When doing the work of God we must abide by His plans!

Account for the Presence of God in Every Situation

Finally, there came a time when the tabernacle was completed.

Then the cloud covered the tent of meeting, and the glory of the Lord filled the tabernacle. And Moses was not able to enter the tent of meeting because the cloud settled on it, and the glory of the Lord filled the tabernacle. Throughout all their journeys, whenever the cloud was taken up from over the tabernacle, the people of Israel would set out. But if the cloud was not taken up, then they did not set out till the day that it was taken up. For the cloud of the Lord was on the tabernacle by day, and fire was in it by night, in the sight of all the house of Israel throughout all their journeys. (Exod. 40:34–38)

From this moment on, every issue of Israel's life turned on whether God was in it. Every bit of progress was based upon the presence of the cloud, which indicated the presence of God.

Once the tabernacle was finished and the glory of the Lord filled the place, Moses was not able to enter into the tent. There is no room for God and man on the same stage. You can generally assume that the glory of God has departed when people start seeking credit or trying to give others credit for the work that God alone has done.

Moses approached the work of God with holy reverence. Nothing was done with a careless, easygoing or irreverent fashion. When God is mightily present in anything, there is no room for a person to command attention or to take credit unto himself.

Considering all that Moses had been through and all that he had done on behalf of Israel, one would presume that there would have been a special place of honor for him in the tabernacle. But he was not able to enter it, because the Lord filled the place.

How did Israel know just when to go forward and when to stop on their forty-year pilgrimage? That issue was settled by the presence or the absence of the cloud. That cloud indicated where God was. The children of Israel arose every morning and looked toward the tabernacle to see if God's presence was still there. If the presence was there, they remained where they were; but if God had moved away, they immediately set out to go and camp where God was.

Is it possible that God has moved away from your life and you have stubbornly resisted following Him? Perhaps you care more about His absence than why He may have left or just where He has gone. Going on in the glory of God means that you must account for the presence of God in every situation of your life.

Manley Beasley often reminded his hearers that every problem in life is a call to worship. In other words, in each situation of life you need to find God. You should ask, "Where is God?" Make your way to Him. And then worship Him.

I was once preaching a revival crusade in a church where it seemed God had been absent for a long time. The crusade itself, however, was highly organized right down to the smallest detail. When I complimented the pastor about the efficient organization, he responded offhandedly, "The way we have this thing organized we are going to have revival, whether God wants us to or not."

How wrong he was! No amount of human effort can substitute for the presence of God nor will God bless anyone who assumes that a life or ministry can succeed without Him.

It is worthy of note that when God's presence moved off of the tabernacle, it often did not move to a place that appeared more conveniently situated for the children of Israel. How easy it would have been to remark, "We have more water where we are." Or, "The climate is better here." Or, "You know, we have had our tents here for three years; we are pretty well established." Or, "We have come to a mutual agreement with the enemies around us." Israel must have been tempted to make excuses for not moving on with God, but, by experience, they had learned that the issue is not the provision we have but whether we have the presence of God.

If the glory is gone from your life, if there is no obvious sense of His presence with you today, if His hand seems to have been taken away, if life has become hard, then it is time for a meeting with the Lord. Whatever you do, whatever radical adjustment it requires of your schedule, do not assume that there is any future in going on without Him.

It is the presence of God you should desire more than all else. It is worth searching for. It is worth staying in the search until you find it. And once God blesses you with the restoration of His glory, it is worth going on in such a fashion that you have both the vital and the visible signs that He is with you. Welcome to the journey! Welcome on the pathway to God's presence!

10

The Handy Tool
Gets Used the Most

"Today, if you hear his voice, do not harden your hearts." (Heb. 4:7)

My grandfather was a preacher, expert wood-craftsman and master of the teachable moment. He was also a patient mentor who taught me many of life's greatest lessons as I worked beside him in the woodshop.

On one occasion he watched with amusement as I fumbled around searching for a tool he had asked me to hand him. As I grasped one strange-looking tool after the other, he broke the silence.

"Never mind," he said with a wry smile, "I just got the job done with this old screwdriver."

As he held the screwdriver up for me to see, he continued. "Tommy, I didn't use this old screw-driver because it was the best tool for the job but because it was close to my hand. It is the handy tool that always gets used the most."

Laying the screwdriver on the workbench, my grandfather then drove home his lesson. "You know, there are a lot of men out in this world who are perfectly equipped to do mighty exploits for God. But in the end, God will always use the man who stays close to Him. Your job is to stay close to God. It's the handy tool God uses most."

Coming to the close of our study of Moses and his determination to only go forward with the assurance of God's presence, it will be wise to remember my grandfather's admonition. As in Moses' case, it is imperative that we remain "handy" to God. That is the only way we can journey forward in life with a continued sense of His mighty presence.

Israel's idolatrous worship under the leadership of Aaron was not their first faithless act on the journey toward Canaan. Nor would it be their last. Psalm 95 reminds us of a later moment of disobedience so egregious that it cost an entire faithless generation their privilege of entering the Promised Land (you may read the account of the event in Numbers 13 and 14 too). Years later, when urging his readers not to forfeit their privilege of "rest" in Christ, the author of Hebrews recalled both that event and David's record of it. "Today," he wrote, "if you hear his voice, do not harden your hearts" (Heb. 3:7–8; 4:7).

What specific actions can you take to remain handy to God and avoid hardening your heart?

Hear!

There is no discipline in the believer's life more important than learning to hear the Master's voice. And where can you best learn the voice of your Great Shepherd? In God's Holy Word, as you faithfully and attentively listen day by day.

For many years, I have sought to remind others that **the plans of God are revealed to the man or woman of God by the Spirit of God and through the Word of God**. That is what Paul was saying as he wrote "All Scripture is breathed out by God and profitable for teaching, for reproof, for correction, and for training in righteousness, that the man of God may be complete, equipped for every good work" (2 Tim. 3:16–17).

My mentor E. F. "Preacher" Hallock was accustomed to reminding his congregation that if you were forced to choose between reading the Bible and praying, it would be far better to read the Word than pray. You do not have to make that choice, of course, but if you did, it would be far better for you to hear what God is saying than for God to hear what you are saying.

Heed!

It is one thing to hear the voice of God as He speaks by His Spirit and through His Word, but it is a far different thing to do what He says. At Kadesh Barnea, Israel heard two reports from the spies who had returned from Canaan. Ten men reported what *they saw* and their report struck fear in the hearts of the Israelites. Joshua and Caleb reported what *God said* and became the only two of their generation to enter the Promised Land forty years later.

Jesus said that obedience was the evidence of genuine faith. "Not everyone who says to me, 'Lord, Lord,' will enter the kingdom of heaven, but the one who does the will of my Father who is in heaven" (Matt. 7:21). And the writer of Hebrews reminds us in the often-quoted roll call of the faithful (Heb.11) that faith is not merely a matter of thought or feeling. Faith is acting on the revealed will of God (Abel *offered*, Enoch *pleased God*, Noah *constructed an ark*, Abraham *went out*, etc.).

Hurry!

"Today!" reads the text in Hebrews. This is the obvious time, the only time and the opportune time to hear and obey God as He calls you to follow Him on the pathway where you will enjoy His presence.

Israel was in no hurry to follow the Lord's urgent appeal as it was being voiced by Joshua and Caleb. And God responded by consigning that faithless and disobedient generation to forty years of wandering and the ultimate death of all but the two faithful spies.

It is worth noting that, after a night of reflection and remembrance, Israel decided that they would follow God after all. But in those *overnight hours* the door to Canaan closed to them forever. Never would the opportunity to live in Canaan be theirs. They did not *hurry* to obey God. Obedience is not obedience unless it is *immediate*.

God Is Calling!

The very fact that you hold this book in your hand and have read to this closing paragraph is an indication that God is calling you to join Him on the pathway. He is urging you to become the *handy tool* at His disposal, someone He can trust with an awesome sense of His mighty presence. But you must *hurry*! The testimony of Scripture is that delayed obedience is always costly. Do you hear Him? If so, run to meet Him on the pathway to God's presence.

This book was produced by CLC Publications. We hope it has been life-changing and has given you a fresh experience of God through the work of the Holy Spirit. CLC Publications is an outreach of CLC Ministries International, a global literature mission with work in over fifty countries. If you would like to know more about us, we invite you to contact us at:

CLC Ministries International
PO Box 1449
Fort Washington, PA 19034

E-mail: mail@clcusa.org
Website: www.clcpublications.com

- - - - - - - - - - - - - - - - - - -

DO YOU LOVE GOOD CHRISTIAN BOOKS?
Do you have a heart for worldwide missions?

You can receive a FREE subscription to
CLC's newsletter on global literature missions

Order by e-mail at:

clcworld@clcusa.org
or mail your request to:

**PO Box 1449
Fort Washington, PA 19034**

READ THE REMARKABLE STORY OF
the founding of
CLC INTERNATIONAL

Leap of Faith

"Any who doubt that Elijah's God still lives ought to read of the money supplied when needed, the stores and houses provided, and the appearance of personnel in answer to prayer." —Moody Monthly

Is it possible that the printing press, the editor's desk, the Christian bookstore and the mail order department can glow with the fast-moving drama of an "Acts of the Apostles"?

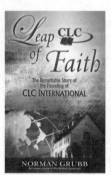

Find the answer as you are carried from two people in an upstairs bookroom to a worldwide chain of Christian bookcenters multiplied by nothing but a "shoestring" of faith and by committed, though unlikely, lives.

trade paper: 978-0-87508-650-7
e-book: 978-1-61958-055-8

To order your copy of *Leap of Faith*

You may order by:
Phone: 1-215-542-1240
E-mail: orders@clcpublications.com
Mail: PO Box 1449
     Fort Washington, PA 19034

Discount Code: LoF 650
Reg. Price: $~~11.99~~
Special Mission Price: $5.40
Shipping in US: $4.00
You pay: $9.40

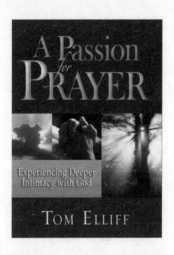

A PASSION FOR PRAYER

Tom Elliff

Of all the disciplines of the Christian life, prayer is perhaps the most neglected.

Yet Jesus' brief earthly life was permeated with it. *A Passion for Prayer* seeks to help you develop—or deepen— your communion with God. Drawing on personal experience and God's Word, Pastor Tom Elliff shares principles for daily coming before the throne of grace.

Trade Paper
Size 5^1/$_4$ x 8, Pages 252
ISBN: 978-1-936143-03-0 - $12.99
ISBN (*e-book*): 978-1-936143-26-9 - $9.99

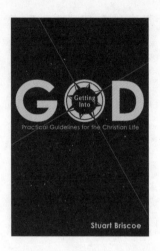

GETTING INTO GOD

Stuart Briscoe

Stuart Briscoe's *Getting into God* will take you through the basic elements of biblical study, prayer and witnessing. Whether you are a new Christian or one simply wanting to get back to the basics of your faith, this book offers some basic instruction on the "practicalities of Christian experience."

Trade Paper
Size 5^1/$_4$ x 8, Pages 144
ISBN: 978-1-61958-152-4 - $11.99
ISBN (*e-book*): 978-1-61958-153-1 - $9.99